# Nuts & Bolts

# Nuts & Bolts

A Practical Guide for
Explaining and Defending
the Catholic Faith

## Tim Staples

**Basilica Press**
SAN DIEGO

Published by Basilica Press
Post Office Box 675205
Rancho Santa Fe, California 92067
www.basilica.com
(888) 396-2339

Cover design by Kinsey Caruth
99 00 01 02 03 15 14 13 12 11 10 09 08 07 06 05 04 03 02 01

Printed in the United States of America ∞
ISBN 0–9642610–2–2

Basilica Press is a division of the Missionaries of Faith Foundation.

# Contents

5

# Foreword

The science of apologetics deals mainly with clearing up misconceptions. Much like the tow-trucks and bulldozers that fan out after a hurricane, clearing fallen trees, downed power lines, and other debris from the roadways, apologists perform the task of removing the debris that can block a person from becoming Catholic.

There are many kinds of obstacles. Some people remain outside the Catholic Church out of basic, well-meaning ignorance. Many converts to the Church have related to me how simple misunderstandings about what the Catholic Church teaches were often to blame for delaying their conversions. They simply didn't realize what the Church taught, and assumed that what they had heard about Catholics was true (such as the common misconception that Catholics have religious statues and images for the purpose of worshipping them). For these people, apologetics removes the blockage of misconception and shows what Catholics really believe.

In other cases, apologetics is a tool for demonstrating that the magisterium of the Church teaches something altogether different from what some Catholics may believe. This is often seen when it comes to issues such as contraception, or the sacrament of holy orders being reserved to men alone. There are, sadly, Catholics running around these days who firmly believe, and encourage others around them to believe, that contraception is okay and that someday women will be allowed to be priests. This situation leads to confusion and misunderstandings, since some non-Catholics are fooled into thinking the Catholic Church is doctrinally "divided" or that it has (or will) change its doctrines once enough people agitate for it. When these situations arise, apologetics is useful for demonstrating not just what the Church teaches on a given issue, but why its teachings aren't up for grabs, why the "majority rules" mindset does not hold sway in doctrinal matters.

More often than not, apologetics is most useful in situations where non-Catholics know exactly what the Catholic Church teaches, and they simply disagree with those teachings. There's no ambiguity here, no problem with the scandal of lukewarm or heterodox Catholics misleading by example. No, typically, apologetics is just a direct correction of error, and it's in this aspect that this book, *Nuts & Bolts*, will prove so useful to the reader.

Catholic apologist Tim Staples deals with the most common variety of arguments against the Catholic Church's teachings that come from Evangelical Protestants, Mormons, Jehovah's Witnesses, and even secularists. Each of these groups has their own particular set of objections, and this book shows you how to deal with fourteen very common ones.

Like a bulldozer, each chapter pushes past standard misconceptions, clearing the path for the mind and heart to draw closer to Christ and His Church. The different apologetics issues you'll read about here are presented in "real life" situations — allowing us to see not just what to say, but how to say it, and in what order to say them.

The old adage is certainly true: "If the only tool you have is a hammer, you will tend to approach every problem as if it were a nail." Now, in this book, you have a whole set of new tools to help you explain and defend the Catholic Church's teachings: Scriptural and linguistic evidence, historical facts, arguments based on sound logic and, perhaps most important of all, a *proven methodology* for using these tools.

Apologetics is learned largely by trial and error. *Nuts & Bolts* is an important new resource because it distills the trial and error of hundreds of conversations with non-Catholics into a series of tightly focused scenarios that expertly guide you through common situations and subjects you're likely to encounter.

I've been working in the apostolate of apologetics for over a dozen years now and, like Tim Staples (who writes the popular column in *Envoy* magazine that this book is adapted from), I've learned that the sequence, timing, tone, and sincerity of the explanations of the Faith a Catholic may offer a non-Catholic are just as crucial as the explanations themselves. The information is important, yes, but the way in which that information is delivered is equally important. As Frank Sheed, the famed Catholic apologist of this century, once warned, "You can win an argument and in the process drive someone further away from the Church."

After assimilating the apologetics content and technique laid out in the chapters of this book, you'll be a lot less likely to fall prey to the danger Sheed reminds us of. You'll be much better equipped to argue without getting angry, explain without being condescending, and encourage without being pushy. Your ability to explain and share the Catholic Faith will grow and strengthen and bear much good fruit.

— *Patrick Madrid*

# Introduction

If someone told me fourteen years ago that I would be defending the veracity of the Catholic Church through speaking, writing and the media all over the world one day, I would have laughed — assuming this to be a feeble attempt at humor. If this person insisted this was a prophetic word from God I would have probably started casting out demons! (I was very Pentecostal in those days.) Yet, here I am fourteen years later defending the Catholic Faith through writing, speaking and the media all over the world! "O the depth of the riches and wisdom and knowledge of God! How unsearchable are his judgments and how inscrutable his ways!" (Rom. 11:33)

Let me give you a little of my background. I was raised Baptist in Falls Church, Virginia and it was always understood in my life that the Catholic Church was in error. From the time I was "saved" when I was ten, it was a given that Catholics needed to get "saved the Bible way". My boyhood heroes (along with my sports idols like Mohammed Ali, Rod Carew, and yes, O. J. Simpson) were Billy Graham and my pastor, Eugene Foreman. In fact, if I couldn't be a champion boxer, pro football or baseball player, I wanted to be a preacher some day like Billy Graham and Pastor Foreman.

In my teen years I got away from the Faith, but when I was eighteen I came back to the Christ of my Youth through some wonderful brothers and sisters in the Assemblies of God Church. I rededicated my life to Christ and sensed the same "calling" in my life I had when I was ten. I wanted to be a preacher and I had a particular desire to "minister" to Catholics.

I suppose it was this very desire to "minister" to Catholics that served as the catalyst for me to be where I am today. I say this because it was while I was trying to get a poor misguided Catholic "saved" that I discovered the true Catholic Faith I now know and love. I met a Catholic who knew his Faith and for the first time in my life I found myself being "out-Bibled" by a Catholic!

I will forever be grateful for my Bible-quoting Catholic friend, Matthew Dula. If he did not allow the Holy Spirit to work in his life fourteen years ago, I may not be enjoying the greatest gift in the universe, the most Blessed Sacrament, today. What Matthew Dula had the uncanny ability to do was give succinct, reasonable and very biblical responses to me on the various issues I would raise with him. If there is one thing we have need of in the Church today, it is people who are able to do just that! Give succinct, reasonable, biblical responses for our Catholic Faith. And that is precisely what this book is for.

For the last two and a half years, I have been a contributing editor for *Envoy* magazine. My column, called "Nuts & Bolts," presents real-life scenarios wherein I help the reader to be able to do just what Matt Dula did for me. I help them to take someone step by step from skepticism to an understanding of what the Catholic Church teaches on a given subject. The reader gets involved in the intellectual process and line of thought underlying many of the misconceptions about our precious Catholic Faith. Most of these scenarios are based on actual experiences I have had in my own life.

We have found the response to these articles to be very positive; hence, the idea for this book was born. Patrick Madrid, the Editor-in-Chief of *Envoy*, suggested we put some of these scenarios together into book form to help our people be better witnesses for our Lord and the true Faith.

It is my prayer that this book will be just that for you. I pray it will help you to become a better, more effective witness and a true blessing to all those around you. May God bless you.

# 1

# Is Jesus Christ God?

*A response to Jehovah's Witnesses' arguments against the divinity of Christ*

## Scenario

Jehovah's Witnesses come to your door on a Saturday afternoon. After a few moments of conversation, one of them spots the crucifix on your wall and remarks, "It's interesting that Catholics believe that Jesus was God. Did you know that the Bible actually teaches that Jesus was not God?"

This "did you know" question is designed to throw you off balance. If you answer with a "no," you appear ignorant and you've given them an invitation to control the discussion. If you say "yes," you've aligned yourself with their heresy. Instead of a "yes" or "no," turn the question back on them and take control of the conversation.

## Your response

"That's an odd point of view. Didn't you know the Bible teaches that Jesus is God?"

Now you have to make good on your claim. Have the following Bible verses (the ones they'll use and the ones you'll use) highlighted in your Bible for easy reference.

## Step One

Ask the Witnesses to read the passages they think dis-
prove Christ's divinity. Here are several they'll use and responses you can give:

*John 14:28* — Jesus says, "The Father is greater than I."

The Father is "greater" than the incarnate Christ in
terms of position because Christ's humanity is a creation,
though in His divinity He is equal to the Father.

*Hebrews 2:9* says that Jesus was made for a while "lower
than the angels" at the Incarnation.

Matthew 11:11 says there has never been a man "greater
than John the Baptist: yet he that is least in the kingdom
of heaven is greater than he." Does this mean John does
not have a human nature? Does this mean those in heaven,
who are greater than John, have a different nature?

If John the Baptist is the greatest man to ever live, and if
Jesus was just a man, does that mean John the Baptist was
greater than Jesus, superior to Him by nature? Does that
mean Jesus and John could not both have had a human
nature?

*John 17:3* — "And this is eternal life, that they know You
the only true God, and Jesus Christ whom You have sent."
The Witnesses will argue that Jesus can't be God if the
Father is the "only true God," and they will point out that
Christ was praying to God here.

God the Father is "the only true God." This statement is completely in harmony with the Catholic doctrine of the Trinity: One God in three Persons. Christ's statement does not entail a denial that He too is God.

Christ was affirming the monotheism of the Jews, that there is only one God. This monotheism is the basis of the Trinity.

Christ is true God and true man (John 1:1, 14; Col. 2:9; John 8:58 & Ex. 3:14), and as a man, He prayed to the Father.

*John 20:17* — "I ascend to My Father and to your Father, to My God and to your God." How can the Father be His 'God' if Christ is God? How can God have a God?"

Say, "I believe that Jesus is both God and man. Here, he speaks in reference to His human nature. As a man the Father is His God — just as He is ours. He calls the Father His God because He is His God whom He worships, prays to and needs in His life just as we do."

This verse is a clear reference to the Hypostatic Union of Christ (He was fully God and man).

*Revelation 3:14* — "These are the words of the Amen, the faithful and true witness, the source of God's creation."

Notice the text does not say Christ was created. The Greek word translated as "source" or "origin" is *arche*. It connotes "the eternal source of all that is."

In Revelation 21:6 Jehovah is called the "Alpha and Omega, the beginning and the end . . . I shall be His God and He shall be My Son." But Jesus is called the "Alpha and Omega, the beginning and the end" in Revelation

22:13. Ask the Witness how Jesus and Jehovah can both be the "Alpha and the Omega." Also ask if this means that Jehovah God had a "beginning," because *arche* is used to describe Him? Here *arche* means "the source of all being." Jesus is the source of the creation of God because he is the creator of all things. John 1:1–3 says Jesus (the Word) created "all things . . . and without Him was made nothing that was made."

If Christ was created, He would have had to have created Himself, which is impossible.

*Colossians 1:15–17* — Jesus is called the "first-born of all creation. For in Him were all things created . . . He is before all and by Him all things were created." JWs think this means Jesus is the first created being.

"First-born" here does not refer to time, but to preeminence. It is a title given by a father to his son. Isaac, Jacob and Ephraim received the blessing of the "first-born," though they were not biologically the first sons born to their parents.

The text doesn't say Jesus was created. If so, St. Paul would have said Jesus created all other things, but he did not. Jesus is the Creator of all things. He is God. He is given the title "first-born" as the title of His preeminence and because He is eternally begotten by the Father.

Ask the JWs if they agree that Colossians 1:15–17 means that Christ created everything. They'll say yes. Then show them Isaiah 44:24: "This is what the Lord says, your Redeemer who formed you in the womb: 'I am the Lord, who has made all things, who alone stretched out the heavens, who spread out the earth by myself.'" Ask them why, if

Christ created "all things," it says that the Lord God — the Hebrew word used here is Yahweh (Jehovah) — did it by Himself.

## Step Two

Tell the Witnesses you believe God is not a God of confusion, but of order and truth. Since He inspired Scripture (*2 Tim. 3:16*), Scripture cannot contradict itself. Quote the following verses and show that only the Catholic position harmonizes all of the texts.

*John 1:1–3* — "In the beginning was the Word, the Word was with God, and the Word was God . . . All things were made by Him: and without Him was made nothing that was made."

Before you bring up this verse, ask the JWs if they believe there are false gods. They will say yes. Then ask them to read John 1:1 from their Bible, which changes the passage to read, "the Word was a god" (see below). Then ask if Christ is the "true" God or a "false" God. They will say a "true" god, but that He is not the One True Almighty God. Then ask them how they explain that Jehovah God commands us to have no other God besides Him (Ex. 20:3). Christ is either the One True God, or He is a false god (cf. Is. 43:10, 44:6–8; John 17:3; 1 Cor. 8:4; 1 Tim. 2:5; James 2:19).

Christ is here clearly identified as God, the Creator of all things. Notice that Genesis 1:1 says "In the beginning God created" everything in the universe. This means Christ is God.

The JWs will respond that the Greek text actually says "the Word was a god"; meaning, Jesus is not the one true God (Jehovah); He was "godlike," but still just a man. They argue that because the Greek definite article *ho* (the) is not used before the Greek word for God (*theos*), when referring to Jesus, He cannot be the God, Jehovah. There are defects with this argument.

First, in this passage the word *theos* is a predicate nominative, and according to Koine Greek grammar rules, predicate nominatives do not take the definite article.

Second, the JW's are inconsistent. Their New World Translation Bible translates *theos* (without the definite article *ho*) as "Jehovah" or "God" numerous times (cf. Matt. 5:9, 6:24; Luke 1:35, 2:40; John 1:6, 12, 13, 18; Rom. 1:7, 17, 18; Titus 1:1). The reason they won't translate it that way in John 1:1 is because to do so would shatter their claim that Christ is not God.

Third, Christ is called *ho theos* (the God) elsewhere in Scripture. For example: "But to the Son [the Father] saith, 'Thy throne, O God (*ho theos*) is for ever and ever'" (Heb. 1:8; see also Titus 2:13, where the definite article *tou* [the genitive singular form of *ho*] precedes the phrase "Great God and Savior"; and "Thomas answered, and said to [Jesus]: 'My Lord and My God'" (John 20:28). The Greek reads: *ho kurios mou kai ho theos mou* ("the Lord of me and the God of me"). If the Witnesses argue that in John 20:28 Thomas was exaggerating about Jesus, point out that if Jesus was not God, Thomas would have been blaspheming and Jesus would have rebuked him, but He didn't — He clearly approves of what Thomas said.

The JWs argue that Thomas referred to Jesus as "Lord" and then to the Father as "God," you respond that there is no evidence for this in the text and Thomas was directly addressing Jesus, not the Father.

*Revelation 22:6* — "And the Lord God of the spirits of the prophets (*ho kurios ho theos*) sent His angel to show His servants the things which must be done shortly."

Who is the Lord God who sent His angel? The Witnesses will say it is Jehovah, but Revelation 22:16 (just ten verses later) says: "I Jesus have sent my angel, to testify to you these things in the Churches." Jesus is "the Lord God of the spirits of the prophets" spoken of in verse 6.

*Luke 12:8–9* — "And I tell you, every one who acknowledges Me before men, the Son of man also will acknowledge before the angels of God; but he who denies Me before men will be denied before the angels of God."

Matthew 13:41 says, "The Son of man will send His angels, and they will gather out of His kingdom all causes of sin and all evildoers." Jesus and God are synonymous.

Genesis 18:25 and Joel 3:12 — Jehovah is the Judge of the world.

Matthew 25:31–46, John 5:27, 9:39; Romans 14:10; 2 Corinthians 5:10; and 2 Timothy 4:1 say that Jesus Christ is the Judge of the world. How can Jesus and Jehovah both be the supreme Judge?

*Exodus 3:13–18* — "Then Moses said to God, 'If I come to the people of Israel and say to them, "The God of your fathers has sent me to you," and they ask me, "What is His Name?" what shall I say to them?' God said to Moses, 'I am who I am.'. . . 'Say this to the people of Israel, "I am has sent me to you. . . The Lord, the God of your fathers, the God of Abraham, the God of Isaac, and the God of Jacob, has sent me to you." This is My Name for ever, and thus I am to be remembered throughout all generations.' "

The Hebrew consonants for the divine name, I am, are YHWH. By inserting the first three vowels for the Hebrew title for God, Adonai, and corrupting the pronunciation, the term JEHOVAH is made. Ask the Witnesses if "Jehovah" (I am) is the Name of the one true God.

Ask the Witnesses if they agree that using the divine Name in vain, or applying it to oneself, would be considered blasphemy in the Old Testament (cf. Ex. 20:7; Deut. 5:11). Ask them what the penalty for doing this would be (cf. Lev. 24:16).

In John 8:21–59 Jesus repeatedly claims the divine name "I am" for Himself. The Jews understood that He was calling Himself God and wanted to stone Him for blasphemy (cf. John 5:18, 8:59, 10:30–36). Ask the Witnesses why the Jews would seek to stone Jesus if He wasn't claiming to be God, especially since execution by stoning was reserved by Jewish Law for only a few crimes.

*Exodus 20:10* — "But the seventh day is the Sabbath of the Lord your God."

Jesus calls himself "The Lord of the Sabbath" in Mark 2:28, thus identifying Himself as God. Cf. Isaiah 8:13 (referred to in 1 Peter 3:15) and Joel 2:31–32 (quoted in Acts 2:20–21 and Romans 10:13).

*Acts 20:28* — "Take heed to yourselves and to all the flock, in which the Holy Spirit has made you overseers, to care for the church of God which he obtained with His own Blood."

Ask the Witnesses when Jehovah ever shed His own Blood. Ask them if Christ shed His own Blood for the Church. If they argue that this passage should read "by the Blood of His own Son," tell them the Greek word son (*huios*) does not appear. It reads: *periepoiesato dia tou haimatos tou idiou.*

Finally, point out the many references where Christ is said to have been slain and shed His Blood for the Church (cf. Matt. 28:27–28; Mark 14:24; Luke 20:20; Rev. 5:6). Point out to them Revelation 5:9: "Worthy art Thou to take the scroll and to open its seals, for Thou wast slain and by Thy Blood didst ransom men for God . . ." This clearly refers to Christ as God.

# 2

# Finders Keepers?

*The Evangelical notion that Christians can't lose
their salvation is unbiblical*

## Scenario

You're discussing religion with an Evangelical friend.
For twenty minutes you've responded as best you can to her
pointed arguments against Catholic doctrines like Mary's
perpetual virginity, praying to saints, venerating statues,
and purgatory. She's unconvinced. You're frustrated. It
doesn't look like there's much of a chance you'll agree
on anything.

Then comes the jackpot question. "Look," she says
earnestly, "we can disagree about many things, but what's
most important is that we know we can be saved by Jesus
Christ. Tell me, if you were to die tonight, do you know
for sure if you'd go to heaven?"

This is the "all-important" question for Evangelical and
Fundamentalist Protestants. Although your friend is completely sincere in asking this question (as she's been coached
to do by her pastor and the anti-Catholic radio preacher
she listens to in the afternoon), you realize that if you don't
answer correctly, you'll walk into a sort of theological am-
bush.

If you respond that Christians can't, apart from a special revelation from God, have metaphysical or absolute certainty concerning their salvation, a completely biblical and theologically precise answer, your Evangelical friend will gleefully spring a "trap" on you, based on 1 John 5:13: "These things I write to you, that you may know you have eternal life, you who believe in the name of the Son of God."

"See?" she smiles confidently. "The Bible disagrees with you!" She then proceeds to inform you that if you "confess with thy mouth the Lord Jesus, and believe in thy heart that God hath raised him up from the dead, thou shalt be saved. For, with the heart, we believe unto justice; but, with the mouth, confession is made unto salvation" (Rom. 10:9–10).

"It's simple, really. Salvation in Christ is a free gift that God is just waiting to give you, if you'll open your heart to Jesus and accept Him as your personal Lord and Savior. The Catholic Church can't promise you an assurance of salvation, but the Bible says you can have that assurance."

## Your response

"I appreciate your sincerity, but I have to disagree. You're taking those verses of Scripture out of context, making them appear to say something they really don't. Jehovah's Witnesses are equally as confident Jesus is not God, and they can quote plenty of verses (like 1 Timothy 2:5) which seem to imply that Jesus was only human, not human and divine. And we know that the Witnesses are wrong. Right? That's why we have to be careful to take Scripture in context, or we'll fall into the old trap — 'A text without a context is a pretext.'"

Now demonstrate that your friend has in fact taken Scripture out of context.

## Step One

Point out that the Greek word in 1 John 5:13 meaning "you may know" is *eidete* (a derivative of *oida*). This term does not necessarily imply an absolutely certain knowledge. The same is true in English and other languages. We use the verb "to know" in more than one way. For example, I could say I know I'm going to get an A on my Greek exam tomorrow. Does that mean I have an absolute certainty of this? No. In fact, I could get a B or worse. In this instance, the verb "I know" means I have confidence I'll get an A on my exam because I have studied the material thoroughly and I know it well. In other words, I have a moral certitude, as opposed to an absolute certitude.

The context of 1 John shows that this broader sense is how *eidete* is used in chapter 5, verse 13. In the very next verses (14–15), St. John says, "And we have this confidence in Him, that if we ask anything according to His will He hears us, and if He hears us we know (Greek: *oidamen;* a derivative of *oida*) that what we have asked him for is ours." Ask your friend if this means she has absolute certainty she'll receive whatever she asks for when she makes specific requests of God in prayer. Obviously, she can't have absolute certainty. Also, we must remember that God is our sovereign Lord, and we trust Him to answer our prayers in the way that is best for us. But sometimes (perhaps often) what we just know is best for us is not, in fact, what's really best for us. God often answers our prayers in a very different way from what we had asked for. So when St. John says, "If we ask anything according to His will He hears us, and if He hears us we know that what we have asked Him for is ours," He is making clear that our knowing is purely conditional on unforeseen factors, not some sort of absolute assurance that, "what we have asked Him for is ours."

Next, quote 1 John 3:21–22: "Beloved, if our hearts do not condemn us, we have confidence in God and receive from Him whatever we ask, because we keep His commandments and do what pleases Him." Here St. John speaks of our having "confidence" that we will receive what we pray for. Here again, this is not a confidence equivalent to an absolute assurance. Furthermore, ask your friend if she is certain she's completely fulfilling the requirements of that verse. Could she have done or be doing things that do not please God? Christ warned that at the Last Judgment, many unrighteous people will be shocked to discover that conduct they thought was acceptable is not, in fact, acceptable to the Lord (Matt. 25:41–46).

## Step Two

The Bible says salvation depends on several things, not just the simple believe/confess formula your friend holds to. Point out that in 1 John, St. John is speaking to Christians (i.e., believers who had accepted Christ as their Lord and Savior (cf. chapter 2:12–14), when he says, "If we say we are without sin, we deceive ourselves, and the truth is not in us. If we confess our sins, He is faithful and just and will forgive our sins and cleanse us from every wrongdoing" (1 John 1:8–9). Notice that St. John includes himself in this category by using the word "we." Ask what would happen if she did not confess her sins. What would happen if she confessed with her mouth but wasn't truly repentant? Would God forgive her anyway? If she says yes, she contradicts the biblical passages that say unrepented sin will not be forgiven and nothing sinful or unclean can enter into heaven (cf. Hab. 1:13; Rev. 21:8–9, 27).

St. John also says, "Let what you heard from the beginning remain in you. If what you heard from the beginning remains in you, then you remain in the Son and in the Father" (1 John 2:24). This if/then construction shows that there is an alternative to "remaining in the Son and the Father." That alternative, naturally, is not remaining in them. In other words, these Christians are being told that it's possible for them to choose not to remain in Him.

St. John makes a distinction between mortal and venial sins in 1 John 5:16–17. He explains that "all wrongdoing is sin," but that some types of sin are "mortal" (Greek: *pros thanaton* = unto death), while there are other sins that are "venial" (Greek: *me pros thanaton* = not unto death). The one who is born of God does not commit mortal sin. If he does, he is "cut off" from the body, as St. Paul describes in Romans 11:22–24 and Galatians 5:4; St. Peter also mentions this in 2 Peter 2:20–22. Christ provided the sacramental means by which a person who commits a grave sin and subsequently repents may be restored to fellowship with God and the Church (cf. John 20:21–23).

## Step Three

Explain that if one can lose his salvation, then salvation cannot be assured absolutely. Remember, we're not talking about a few isolated examples of our salvation being contingent upon our remaining in God's grace. There are "ifs" and contingency clauses all over the New Testament regarding salvation, almost all of them of St. Paul warning Christians. Quote the following verses to make your point.

Romans 11:22: "See, then, the kindness and severity of God: severity towards those who fell (i.e., from salvation: 11:11–21), but God's kindness to you, provided you remain in His kindness, otherwise you too will be cut off."

Other clear contingency clauses pertaining to salvation are Matthew 10:22–32; Luke 12:41–46; 1 Corinthians 15:1–2; Colossians 1:22–23; Hebrews 3:6, 14; and Revelation 2:10, 25–26, 3:1–5, 22:18–19.

2 Peter 2:20–22: "For if, flying from the pollutions of the world, through the knowledge of our Lord and Savior Jesus Christ, they be again entangled in them and overcome: their latter state is become unto them worse than the former. For, that of the true proverb has happened to them: The dog is returned to his vomit: and the sow that was washed, to her wallowing in the mire."

Scripture can't get much clearer than that in explaining that one can lose his salvation. But your friend might respond, "The person spoken of here never really knew the Lord, he only knew about the Lord." You should respond by pointing out that the Greek word used here for knowledge is *epignosei*. The root word, *gnosei*, means knowledge, but a particular kind of knowledge. We mentioned *oida* above. This term refers to an intellectual knowledge. *Gnosei*, on the other hand, denotes knowledge that comes from experience. Further, the word here in 2 Peter 2:20 has the prefix *epi*, meaning "full," making it *epignosei* which would translate literally into English as "full experiential knowledge." This points us toward the fact that the sinner spoken of in this text has "escaped the defilements of the world" through a "full experiential knowledge" of Christ Jesus. Only a saving relationship with Christ can have this effect. Is there any other way to "escape the defilements of the world" except by becoming justified in Christ? No. And merely knowing about Jesus isn't enough. Notice too, that the image St. Peter uses in verse 22 is a sow that has been washed in water. He speaks of water baptism in 2 Peter 3:20–21 when he says "This [water of the Great Flood] prefigured baptism which now saves you." The connection between 2 Peter 2:20 and 1 Peter 3:21 is obvious — both passages deal with different elements of salvation.

Ask your friend to read 2 Peter 1:2–4 in order to establish the context for 2 Peter 2:20. Notice that St. Peter begins his letter with a description of believers to whom he is writing: "Grace and peace be multiplied unto you through the knowledge (*epignosei* = full experiential knowledge), of God, and of Jesus our Lord . . . that . . . you might be partakers of the divine nature, after escaping from the corruption that is in the world because of evil desire." The Greek word *apophugentes* ("having escaped from") and the phrase *en to kosmo* ("in the world") describe exactly the condition of being a "born again" Christian: one who has been freed by God's grace from sin and defilement. These are the same words used in 2 Peter 2:20 to describe the one who then goes back to his old sinful state, worse off than before he had accepted Jesus as his savior and was born again. "For they, having escaped (*apophugentes*) the defilements of the world (*tou kosmou*) through the knowledge (*epignosei*) of the Lord Jesus Christ, again become entangled and overcome by them, their last condition is worse than their first."

Now go to Matthew 6:15, where Jesus warns, "If you do not forgive others, neither will your heavenly Father forgive you your transgressions." In other words, the Lord doesn't care how "born again" you may claim to be or how many spiritual experiences you've had. If you don't forgive others, you will not be forgiven of your sins. This warning about losing salvation is repeated in Matthew 19:21–35.

The Bible warns Christians that they can "fall from grace" (Gal. 5:1–5), be "cut off" from salvation (Rom. 11:18–22), have their names removed from the Lamb's book of life (Rev. 22:19–19), by committing certain sins and not repenting of them (cf. Eph. 5:3–5; 1 Cor. 6:9; Gal. 5:19; Rev. 21:6–8). In a chilling reminder of the possibility of losing salvation by separating oneself from Christ, St. Paul adds, "I drive my body and train it, for fear that, after having preached to others, I myself should be disqualified" (1 Cor. 9:27).

## Step Four

Now it's time to discuss the meaning of Romans 10:9–10, which your friend used at the outset of the discussion. "The Bible says that if you believe in your heart and confess Jesus with your mouth, you shall be saved!"

## Your response

"Yes, it does say that, but it doesn't mean that we confess him one time only. The Greek word used here for confess, *homologeitai*, entails our continued confession of Christ throughout our lives. In Matthew 10:22–32 our Lord says,

> You shall be hated by all men for My name's sake, but he that endures until the end shall be saved. Everyone who acknowledges [*homologesei*] Me before men, him will I acknowledge [*homologesei*] before My heavenly Father. But whoever denies Me before others, I will deny before My heavenly Father.

Notice the context is one of holding fast to one's confession of Christ until death (cf. Heb. 4:14, 10:23–26 and 2 Tim. 2:12).

"The Bible is clear that confessing Christ is done not merely by words, but primarily by deeds. Conversely, denying Christ is done primarily by deeds: sins.

"1 Timothy 5:8 'Whoever does not provide for relatives and especially family members, has denied the faith and is worse than an unbeliever' (cf. 1 Tim. 5:11–12, 15). This means denying Christ by one's actions.

"1 Corinthians 6:9 says,

> Do you not know that the unjust will not inherit the kingdom of God? Do not be deceived; neither fornicators nor idolaters nor adulterers nor boy prostitutes nor practicing homosexuals nor thieves nor the greedy nor drunkards nor slanderers nor robbers will inherit the kingdom of God [cf. Eph. 5:3–5; Gal. 5:19; Rev. 21:8–9, 27].

Scripture nowhere says that 'born again' Christians can commit such sins as these, die unrepentant, and still go to heaven anyway."

To salvage her position, your friend might counter with Romans 8:35–37:

What will separate us from the love of Christ? Will anguish, or distress, or persecution, or famine, or nakedness, or peril, or the sword? . . . No, in all these things we conquer overwhelmingly through him who loved us. For I am convinced that neither death, nor life, nor angels, nor principalities, nor present things, nor future things, nor powers nor height, nor depth, nor any other creature will be able to separate us from the love of God which is in Christ Jesus our Lord.

Your friend asks, "Doesn't that verse clearly teach that Christians have eternal security?"

## Your response

Point out that in his list of things that cannot separate us from Christ, he doesn't mention adultery, murder, fornication, etc. Why? Because St. Paul tells us that doing these things will separate us from Christ. This list also excludes the Christian himself. Since God loves us and respects our free will, it is still possible for a Christian to be born again and then later, through his own free choice, separate himself from Christ.

A final warning from St. Paul is in order: "These things happened as examples for us (i.e., born again Christians), so that we might not desire evil things, as they did. Do not become idolaters, as some of them did . . . let us not indulge in immorality, as some of them did. These things happened to them as an example, and they have been written down as a warning to us, upon whom the end of the ages has come. Therefore, whoever thinks he is standing secure should take care not to fall" (1 Cor. 10:6–8, 11–12).

# 3

# "My Flesh Is Real Food"

*Here's a brief, step-by-step way to explain*
*the Real Presence of Christ in the Eucharist*

## Scenario

You're at the annual family reunion barbecue. In the midst of the fun you overhear your cousin Mark (who left the Church in college and now attends a Fundamentalist Baptist church) arguing heatedly about religion with several of your Catholic relatives. He's got his Bible out and is vigorously explaining why the Catholic doctrine of the Eucharist is "unbiblical." "You don't really believe that you eat Jesus when you receive Communion, do you?" he rolls his eyes, shaking his head at the very thought. "It's obvious from Scripture that Jesus was speaking symbolically when He talked about eating His flesh and drinking His blood. He didn't mean that literally." Your relatives are no match for Mark's energy and confidence. And besides, they don't have Bibles with them, so he's pretty much in charge of the conversation — that is, until you walk over and with a big smile you ask, "Mark, if I can show you from the Bible that your argument is wrong and that Christ did teach that He is really present in the Eucharist, will you come back to the Catholic Church?" Mark's sermon stops in mid syllable.

He grins and shakes his head. "There is no way you can prove that from the Bible. And besides, you're a Catholic. Your doctrines don't come from the Bible, anyway."

## Your response

"Well, we'll see about that. But please answer my question. If I can show you from the Bible that the Catholic teaching is true, will you come back to the Church?" "Heck yeah," he snorts, confident your proposition is one he can't lose. "Go ahead and try. But first, answer me this: In John 10:1, Jesus said He is a 'door.' Do you believe He has hinges and a doorknob on His body? In John 15:1, Jesus said He is a 'vine.' Do you take Him literally there? If not, why do you take His words literally in John 6 where He talked about His flesh and blood being like food and drink? You Catholics are inconsistent."

## Step One

Explain that if Jesus was not speaking literally in John 6 ("My flesh is real food; My blood is true drink," etc.), He would have been a poor teacher. After all, everyone listening to Him speak those words understood that He meant them literally. They responded, "How can this man give us His flesh to eat?" In the cases of Jesus saying He is a "door" or a "vine," we find no one asking, "How can this man be a door made out of wood?" or, "How can this man claim to be a plant?" It was clear from the context and the Lord's choice of words in those passages that He was speaking metaphorically. But in John 6 He was speaking literally.

In John 6:41, the Jews "murmured" about Christ's teaching precisely because it was so literal. Christ certainly knew they were having difficulty imagining that He was speaking literally, but rather than explain His meaning as simply a metaphor, He emphasized His teaching, saying, "I am the living bread that came down from heaven. Whoever eats this bread will live forever, and the bread that I will give is My flesh for the life of the world" (John 6:51).

Why would Christ reinforce the literal sense in the minds of His listeners if He meant His words figuratively? Now point out how the Lord dealt with other situations where His listeners misunderstood the meaning of His words. In each case, He cleared up the misunderstanding. For example, the disciples were confused about His statement, "I have meat to eat that you know not of" (John 4:32). They thought he was speaking about physical food — real meat. But He quickly cleared up the misunderstanding with the clarification, "My meat is to do the will of Him that sent Me, that I may perfect his work" (Matt. 4:34; cf. 16:5–12).

Back to John 6. Notice that the Jews argued among themselves about the meaning of Christ's words. He reiterated the literal meaning again: "Amen, Amen, I say to you, unless you eat the flesh of the Son of Man and drink His blood, you do not have life within you" (vv. 53–54). In verse 61 we see that no longer was it just the wider audience but "the disciples" themselves who were having difficulty with this radical statement. Surely, if Christ were speaking purely symbolically, it's reasonable to expect that He would clear up the difficulty even if just among His disciples. But He doesn't. He stands firm and asks, "Does this shock you? What if you were to see the Son of Man ascending to where He was before?" (vv. 62–63). Did Christ "symbolically" ascend into heaven after the Resurrection?

No. As we see in Acts 1:9–10, His ascension was literal. This is the one and only place in the New Testament where people abandon Christ over one of His teachings.

Rather than try to correct any mistaken understanding of His words, the Lord asks His Apostles, "Do you also want to leave?" (verse 67). His Apostles knew He was speaking literally. St. Paul emphasizes the truth of the Real Presence: "Whoever eats the bread or drinks the cup of the Lord unworthily, shall be guilty of the body and blood of the Lord. . . . Whoever eats and drinks without recognizing the body, eats and drinks judgment on himself" (1 Cor. 11:27–29).

If the Eucharist is merely a symbol of the Lord's body and blood, then St. Paul's words here make no sense. For how can one be "guilty of the body and the blood of the Lord" if it's merely a symbol? This Greek phrase for being "guilty of someone's body and blood" (*enokos estai tou somatos kai tou haimatos tou kuriou*) is a technical way of saying "guilty of murder." If the Eucharist is merely a symbol of Christ, not Christ Himself, this warning would be drastically, absurdly overblown.

## Step Two

Next, point out the fact that the "Real Presence" of Christ in the Holy Eucharist was a doctrine believed and taught unanimously by the Church since the time of Christ. The Catholic "literal" sense was always and only the sense in which the early Christians understood Christ's words in John 6. The "figurative" or "metaphorical" sense was never held by the Church Fathers or other early orthodox Christians. This can be proven not just by appealing to the

writings of the Fathers, but also by the fact that ancient
Christian traditions such as the Copts and the Orthodox
Churches also hold and teach the doctrine of the Real Pres-
ence, just as the Catholic Church does. St. Ignatius of An-
tioch, a disciple of St. John the Apostle and successor of
St. Peter as bishop of Antioch, wrote:

> They [the heretics] abstain from the Eucharist and from
> prayer, because they do not confess that the Eucharist is
> the Flesh of our Savior Jesus Christ, Flesh which suffered
> for our sins and which the Father, in His goodness, raised
> up again [*Epistle to the Smyrnaeans* 6 (A.D. 107)].

Even Martin Luther himself admitted that the early
Church was unanimous in the literal interpretation of
Christ's words in John 6:

> Who, but the devil, hath granted such license of wrest-
> ing the words of holy Scripture? Who ever read in the
> Scriptures that my body is the same as the sign of my
> body? . . . It is only the devil, that imposeth upon us by
> these fanatical men. . . . Not one of the Fathers, though
> so numerous, ever spoke [thus] . . . they are all of them
> unanimous.

## Step Three

You can make your case another way. Say, for the sake
of argument, that Christ intended His words in John 6 to
be understood metaphorically. Even if this were granted,
the anti-Catholic argument your cousin Mark is using still
falls apart. Here's why: The phrases "eat flesh" and "drink
blood" did indeed have a symbolic meaning in the Hebrew language and culture of our Lord's time. You can
demonstrate this by quoting passages such as Psalm 27:1–

2, Isaiah 9:18–20, Isaiah 49:26, Micah 3:3, and Revelation 17:6, 16. In each case, we find "eating flesh" and "drinking blood" used as metaphors to mean "to persecute," "to do violence to," "to assault," or "to murder." Now, if Christ were speaking metaphorically, the Jews would have understood him to be making an absurd statement: "Unless you persecute and assault Me, you shall not have life in you. Amen, amen, I say to you, unless you do violence to Me and kill Me, you shall not have life within you." Besides being an absurd understanding of these words, there is one further problem with the "metaphorical" view: Jesus would have been encouraging — exhorting! — His hearers to commit violent mortal sins. If it were immoral, in any sense, for Christ to promise to give us His flesh to eat and His blood to drink, then he could not have commanded us to even symbolically eat and drink His body and blood. Even symbolically performing an immoral act is of its very nature immoral. You can see your explanations are hitting home, but you're not done yet. Mark still has a few arguments left. "Look," he sighs. "You haven't convinced me. After all, Jesus Himself said in John 6:63 that He wasn't speaking literally: 'It is the spirit that gives life, while the flesh is of no avail. The words I have spoken to you are spirit and life.' How do you get around that?"

## Your response

The word "spirit" (Greek: *pneuma*) is never used anywhere in Scripture to mean "symbolic." John 4:24 says God is "spirit" (*pneuma*). Does that mean He is "symbolic?" Hebrews 1:14 tells us that angels are "spirit" (*pneuma*.) Are angels merely symbols? Of course not. You can multiply the examples of the constant use of the word "spirit" as a literal, not figurative, reality. Now point out that *sarx*, the Greek term for "flesh," is sometimes used in the New Testament to describe the condition of our fallen human nature apart from God's grace. For example, St. Paul says that if we are "in the flesh," we cannot please God (cf. Rom. 8:1–14). He also reminds us that, "the natural person does not accept what pertains to the Spirit of God, for to him it is foolishness, and he cannot understand it because it is judged spiritually" (1 Cor. 2:14). Remind Mark that it doesn't require grace to look at Communion as just grape juice and crackers. It does, however, require faith and "spiritual judgment" to see and believe Christ's promise that He would give us His body, blood, soul and divinity under the appearances of bread and wine. The one who is "in the flesh," operating in the realm of mere natural understanding, won't see this truth. Your cousin has a comeback ready. "But Jesus says, 'I am the bread of life. Whoever comes to me will never hunger, and whoever believes in me will never thirst.' I believe this means that coming to Him is what He really means by "eating" and believing in Him is what He really means by "drinking." Not so. Point out that "coming to" and "believing in" Christ are definite requirements for having this life He promises, but not the only ones. It would, after all, be a sacrilege to receive the Eucharist without believing (cf. 1 Cor. 11:27–29). But this doesn't erase the fact that Christ repeatedly said, "My flesh is real food, and My blood is real drink." This literal dimension of the passage can't be explained away by appealing to "coming" and "believing." To do that would be to make the mistake of focusing solely on just one aspect of the Lord's teaching and ignoring the rest of it. Mark is starting to look a little uncomfortable. You're still smiling. He's not. "Wait!" he says. "Leviticus 17:10 condemns eating blood. There's no way Jesus would contradict this. He would have been encouraging cannibalism if He really meant for us to eat His body and drink His blood. That would be immoral."

## Step Four

Acknowledge that Leviticus 17:10 indeed condemns "eating blood." Then say, "If we're going to be consistent with the Levitical Law, then we must also perform animal sacrifices — lambs, pigeons, turtledoves — according to Leviticus 12:8. But as Christians, we are not under the Levitical Law. We're under the 'law of the spirit of life in Christ Jesus' " (Rom. 8:2). Hebrews 7:11–12 tells us the Levitical Law has passed away with the advent of the New Covenant. A New Testament commandment always abrogates an Old Testament commandment. For example, in Matthew 5, the Lord repeatedly uses the formula, "You have heard that it was said (quoting an Old Testament law), But I say unto you . . ." In each instance, Christ supersedes the Old Testament law with a new commandment of His own, such as the commandment against divorce and remarriage, over against Moses' allowance for it in Deuteronomy 24:1 (cf. Matt. 5:21–22, 27–28, 31–32, 33–34, 38–39, 43–44). This is what we see in John 6. The blood prohibition in Leviticus 17:11–12 was replaced by Christ's new teaching in John 6:54: "Unless you eat the flesh of the Son of Man and drink His blood, you shall have no life in you." Eating blood was prohibited in the Old Testament, "Because the life of the flesh is found in the blood" (Lev. 17:11). Blood is sacred and the life of each creature is in its blood. Many pagans thought they could acquire "more" life by ingesting the blood of an animal or even a human being. But obviously this was foolish. No animal or human person has the capacity to do this. But in the case of Christ, it's different. John 6:54 tells us that our eternal life depends on His blood: "Unless you eat the flesh of the Son of Man and drink His blood, you shall have no life in you."

## Step Five

By now Cousin Mark has run out of things to say. Rather than hold him to his promise to become Catholic on the spot, give him a hug, tell him you're praying for his return to the Church and that he's always welcome to come home. Then go get another helping of Aunt Mary's potato salad. You've earned it.

# 4

# "Baptism Now Saves You"

*A mechanic gets his tires rotated by a Catholic who knows how to get born again the "Bible way"*

## Scenario

Its nine o'clock on Saturday morning. You've taken your car to the local garage for new tires and an oil change. Bill, the manager, introduces himself with a broad smile and a firm handshake. As he finishes the paperwork and you're signing on the dotted line, you notice him eyeing the icon of Our Lady of Guadalupe on your T-shirt. Bill asks, "I gather from your T-shirt that you're Catholic. I was raised Catholic, and I respect Catholics, *but . . .*" (You were waiting for that all-significant conjunction.) "I now have a personal relationship with Jesus Christ, one that's not dependent on being a member of a church or denomination." He smiles widely. You nod politely as he tells you how he accepted Jesus Christ as his "personal Lord and Savior," how he was "born again," and how he now attends a Bible teaching church "where the Word is really preached." As he hands you your receipt he pops the question: "Have you been born again?"

*Your response*

As a matter of fact, I have. In fact, I was born again the
Bible way. But before we cover that, I have to tell you that
I find it odd that you left the Catholic Church in order
to find a personal relationship with Jesus. I have a very
personal relationship with Jesus through prayer as well as
through the Church and the sacraments He instituted. He
gave us these gifts so we can know with certainty the truth
He came to preach and experience the divine life of grace in
our lives. My relationship with Jesus couldn't be any more
personal." Bill furrows his brow. "Huh. But I thought you
were Catholic."

"Yes, I'm Catholic, and that's why I was born again the
Bible way. I was born again when I was about three weeks
old — when I was baptized."

Bill frowns slightly and tilts his head to one side, but says
nothing. "Jesus explains what it means to be born again
in John 3:3–5," you explain. "In that text, He teaches us
about the sacrament of baptism." Bill shakes his head. "No.
Baptism doesn't save you, brother. John 3:5 says we must
be born again of water and the Spirit. The water means
amniotic fluid, our first, natural birth through our physical
mothers. But the second birth, being born again, is from
the Holy Spirit. Jesus meant that we are born again accepting Him as our personal Lord and Savior."

Confident that you won't be able to answer him bib-
lically, he awaits your response. Bill is busy running the
garage and he can't spend a lot of time talking with you.
You've got maybe ten minutes in which to share the ba-

sics of what the Bible says about baptism and salvation, so you'll have to work quickly.

## Step One

Go get your Bible from the back seat of your car and ask Bill to show you where in John 3 Jesus mentions "accepting Him as your personal Lord and Savior." He won't be able to because the passage doesn't say anything like that. Explain that he's reading something into a text that is simply not there.

"The Bible way of getting born again," you explain, "is by being baptized in the name of the Father, and of the Son, and of the Holy Spirit. Anything else is unbiblical." Now ask him to look at the context of chapters one through three of the Gospel of John.

First, Christ Himself is baptized (John 1:31–34; cf. Matt. 3:16). When He is baptized, the heavens are opened and the Holy Spirit descends upon Him in the form of a dove. Obviously, Jesus didn't need to be baptized. In fact, St. John the Baptist exclaimed that he needed to be baptized by Christ (cf. Matt. 3:14). The Lord was baptized to show us the way of salvation (cf. Luke 1:77), the way the heavens are opened to us, and the way the Holy Spirit descends upon us.

Second, He performs His first miracle in John 2:1–11 by transforming water into wine. Notice that He used water from "six stone jars . . . for the Jewish rites of purification." According to the Septuagint (Greek) canon of the Old Testament, these ritual purification waters were called *baptismoi,* in essence, the Old Testament's "baptismal" waters (cf. Numbers 19:9–19). The Old Testament rites and sacrifices were only "a shadow of the good things to come" (Heb. 10:1). They could never take away sins. Scripture scholars point out that the number six was often used to denote imperfection. Christ transformed the Old Testament water of "ritual washings" into wine, a symbol of New Covenant perfection (cf. Joel 3:18, Matt. 9:17).

Third, in John 3:22, immediately after Christ's "born again" discourse to Nicodemus, what does He do? He and His disciples go out into the countryside and begin to baptize. Also, in John 4:1–2, His disciples alone are seen baptizing. The Lord most likely baptized His disciples (though this can't be proven, but only inferred from the text), and then they went out and baptized the multitudes.

Let's recap the progression of events in the Gospel of John: Christ is baptized, He elevates and sanctifies the waters of baptism, He gives the "how to be born again" discourse, He baptizes the disciples and commissions them to go out and baptize. Clearly, in view of the context of these passages, Christ's words in John 3 mean that baptism is the way one is born again.

Saying that the "water" spoken of in John 3:5 is amniotic fluid goes way beyond stretching the context of this passage. John 3:5 ("No one can enter the kingdom of God without being born of water and Spirit") is not describing two events, but one. For example, the text doesn't imply something like: "No one can enter the kingdom of God without being first born of water and then born again of spirit." He is speaking of the event of water baptism, the effects of which were depicted for us in His own baptism: He went down into the water, the Holy Spirit descended on Him, the voice of the Father was heard saying, "This is

My beloved Son, with Whom I am well pleased." This is what happens at the sacrament of baptism. We are made right with God, justified, and put into a son/Father relationship.

## Step Two

Ask Bill to show you where the Bible mentions that being born again happens as a result of saying the "Sinners Prayer" and accepting Christ as ones personal Lord and Savior. He will probably quote Romans 10:9–10:

> If you confess with your mouth that Jesus is Lord and believe in your heart that God raised Him from the dead, you will be saved. For one believes with the heart and so is justified; and one confesses with the mouth and so is saved. . . . For anyone who calls on the name of the Lord will be saved [Rom. 10:9–10, 13].

Bill looks at you steadily. "The Bible doesn't explicitly say we're born again by accepting Jesus, but it does say we're saved by professing faith in Him."

"I understand what you're driving at," you say, "and I agree with you that it's necessary to believe in and profess Christ in order to be saved. But, this still doesn't do away with the role of baptism. Let me explain the Catholic teaching on this."

Over the next few minutes, you explain that the initial grace of justification, in the case of adult converts and children above the age of reason, begins with the gift of faith which is entirely unmerited (cf. Eph. 2:8–9). We must then cooperate with this grace (Rom. 11:22), which has been radically augmented and perfected in the sacrament of baptism. A man does not merit anything in this process, but once he is born again the Bible way, by water and spirit in the sacrament of baptism, he can merit rewards from God (cf. Matt. 25; Gal. 4:4–6, 5:1–6, 6:7–8; Rom. 2:6–10).

Next, explain that confessing Christ is an essential part of the process of justification. But baptism is the point at which one receives the initial grace of union with Christ in a perfected sense. The difference is similar to a child's physical birth and development. He is only born once, but thereafter he must grow physically or die.

Regarding Romans 10:9, where it says the one who believes "will be saved," point out that the Greek word *"sozo,"* which means "to save," is used to describe many things necessary for salvation. Here are two examples: The one who "believes and is baptized will be saved" (Mark 16:16); and the one who "endures to the end shall be saved" (Matt. 10:22, 24:13). Similarly, in Romans 10:10 St. Paul says that confession of Christ is made "unto salvation" (KJV). The Greek phrase used here, *"eis soterian,"* means "unto salvation" and is used in the context of St. Peter's admonishing his (born again Christian) audience to "long for the pure spiritual milk, that by it you may grow up to salvation" (1 Peter 2:2).

Similarly, we're told that we must also repent of serious sins: "For godly sorrow produces a repentance that leads to salvation . . ." (2 Cor. 7:10). The fact that we must repent, be baptized, grow, confess Christ and endure until the end in order to be saved indicates that salvation, in regards to us as individuals, is a process, not merely a once for all event. St. Paul is speaking of the initial part of this process in Romans 10:9–13.

Bill responds, quoting from his King James Bible, "What about the part of Romans 10:10 that says, 'With the heart man believes unto righteousness'? You believe and are justified before God. Isn't that being born again?" "Not exactly. Notice that the text you read doesn't say what you said. This belief is much more than just professing faith in Christ one time. In fact, right after St. Paul describes new life in Christ in Romans 6:1–10, he then warns us not to fall back into sin. In verse 16 he declares: Do you not know that if you yield yourselves to any one as obedient slaves, you are slaves of the one whom you obey, either of sin which leads to death, or of obedience which leads to righteousness? The Greek phrase used here, *hupakoes eis dikaiosunen*, means obedience unto righteousness or obedience unto justification."

"Our obedience to Christ (after baptism) leads us unto justification as much as our faith in Christ does. Belief and confession are part of the process of salvation, and we must persevere in both" (cf. Matt. 10:22–33; Luke 9:23; Acts 13:43; Col. 1:22–23; 2 Tim. 2:12; Rev. 2:10).

Next explain that the Bible says that one is incorporated into the Body of Christ through baptism, not by saying the "sinners prayer." Romans 6:3–4 says,

> Are you unaware that we who were baptized into Christ Jesus were baptized into his death? We were indeed buried with Him through baptism into death, so that, just as Christ was raised from the dead by the glory of the Father, we too might live in newness of life.

Galatians 3:27 says, "For all of you who were baptized into Christ have clothed yourselves with Christ." (Cf. Mark 16:16; Acts 2:38, 22:16; 1 Cor. 12:12; Col. 2:11–13; Eph. 4:5.)

## Step Three

Bill thinks for a second. "I think you're confusing spiritual baptism with water baptism. Water baptism can't save you. 1 Corinthians 12:12 says that it is the Spirit that baptizes us into Christ, not some man."

"Yes, I agree," you begin. "The Holy Spirit does incorporate us into Christ, just as the Holy Spirit convince[s] the world of sin and of righteousness and of judgment (John 16:8). But don't forget that the Holy Spirit also uses human instruments to convey the message. For example, St. Paul said, How shall they hear without a preacher? (Rom. 10:14). The same is true for baptism. It is an action of grace performed by the Holy Spirit in conjunction with the human action of the one who baptizes."

"In Acts 2:38 St. Peter exclaimed, 'Repent, and be baptized every one of you in the name of Jesus Christ for the forgiveness of your sins; and you shall receive the gift of the Holy Spirit.' In Acts 22:16, Ananias declared to Saul, who had already professed faith in Christ as Lord in verse 10, 'Why delay? Get up and be baptized and your sins washed away, calling on His name.' 1 Peter 3:20–21 says '[a] few persons, eight in all, were saved through water.' This prefigured baptism which saves you now. It is not a removal of dirt from the body but an appeal to God for a clear conscience, through the Resurrection of Jesus Christ. The passage is clear: Baptism now saves you." You can tell that Bill is shaken by this. He's not as assertive and confident as he was just a short time ago. He says, "But Ephesians 2:8–9 says, For by grace (not by baptism) you have been saved through faith, and this is not of yourselves, it is the gift of God, not of works, lest any man should boast." "Exactly," you respond. "That is the description of the initial grace of salvation that we know comes through baptism." Just then, a mechanic brings your car keys to Bill. As you walk together toward the car, you can almost see the wheels turning in his mind. Clearly, he's reflecting on your answers to his questions.

You decide to take the extra step. "You know, I've got an extra copy of an apologetics booklet here in my car that I'd like to leave with you. It goes into greater depth on the sacrament of baptism and what the Bible says about it. It contains many more Bible verses and even has quotes from the early Church Fathers that show what the early Christians believed about baptismal regeneration. Would you be willing to read it? Maybe we could get together and discuss this issue again sometime."

A moment's pause. "Why not," Bill says. "I've enjoyed our conversation, even though I don't agree with every-thing you said. One thing's for sure, though. I see I need to study this subject more carefully. We'll have to continue this discussion."

"Yes, I'd like that," you smile as you shake hands. "See you in about 3,000 miles."

# 5

# A Discussion That
# Bore Good Fruit

*The biblical evidence that religious statues
and icons are A-Ok in God's Book*

## Scenario

You're at the grocery store shopping. As you're squeezing melons, you spot a young couple over by the carrots.
You can't help but notice their matching "It's a Child, Not
a Choice" T-shirts. As they walk your way, you compliment them on their shirts and comment that you're Catholic, and you appreciate their willingness to witness to the
truth about abortion.

"I was Catholic, then I became a Christian," the man
responds.

"Are you implying that Catholics are not Christians?"
you ask.

You continue almost mindlessly squeezing melons as he
confidently answers, "I could give you many reasons why
Catholics are not Christians, but why don't we start with
idolatry?" His wife reaches into her purse and hands her
husband a small King James Bible.

You think to yourself, "What have I gotten myself into here?" as he turns to Exodus 20:2–5:

> "I am the Lord thy God, which have brought thee out of the land of Egypt, out of the house of bondage. Thou shalt have no other gods before me. Thou shalt not make unto thee any graven image, or any likeness of any thing that is in heaven above, or that is in the earth beneath, or that is in the water under the earth. Thou shalt not bow down thyself to them, nor serve them."

The man looks at you. "How could God make it any clearer? We are not to have 'graven images.' Yet what do you see in every Catholic Church around the world? Graven images! Statues! This is the definition of idolatry. And please, don't try to equate the statues in your churches to carrying a photograph of a loved one in your wallet. In Exodus 20, as well as in Deuteronomy 5:7–8, God specifically says we are not to make images, or statues, in the shape of anything in heaven above, the earth beneath or the water under the earth."

## Your response

At this point, you introduce yourself, shake hands with both of them and ask their names. They are Andy and Alice. You ask Andy and Alice, "What if I could show you in Sacred Scripture, in fact, in your own King James Version, there is nothing wrong with having statues of Jesus, angels and of great men and women of the Faith in our churches and homes? Even further, what if I showed you that God commands His people to make graven, or carved, images, and is pleased with His people when they do? What would you say about the Catholic understanding of statues and images then?"

"First of all," Andy answers, "you won't be able to do that. But even if you could, I would still believe Catholicism is not Christian. There are many more issues we would have to discuss."

"But at least you would acknowledge that you had been wrong about the Church on this issue," you say.

"I suppose," he says reluctantly, "but let's get to the point at hand."

## *Step One*

You explain to Andy that the key is found in verse five of Exodus 20: "Thou shalt not bow down thyself to them, nor serve them." God did not mean the Israelites or we could not have statues. He prohibits serving, or worshipping them. If God meant we are not to have any statues at all of any likeness of any created thing in a strict, absolute sense, then God contradicts Himself. Just five chapters after this statement in Exodus 20, God gives Moses explicit instructions on how to construct the ark of the covenant. This ark was to contain the presence of God and was to be venerated as the holiest place in all of Israel.

> "And thou shalt make a mercy seat of pure gold: two cubits and a half shall be the length thereof, and a cubit and a half the breadth thereof. And thou shalt make two cherubims of gold, of beaten work shalt thou make them, in the two ends of the mercy seat. And make one cherub on the one end, and the other cherub on the other end: even of the mercy seat shall ye make the cherubims on the two ends thereof" [Exodus 25:17–19].

Here God commands Moses to make graven images. Note that in Exodus 20, the commandment said we are not to "make unto thee any graven image, or any likeness of any thing that is in heaven above, or that is in the earth beneath, or that is in the water under the earth." Here we have graven images of angels from "heaven above." Now take Andy and Alice to 1 Kings 6 to see God command Solomon to make images of things in both "heaven above" and "the earth beneath." First, God tells Solomon:

> "Concerning this house which thou art in building, if thou wilt walk in my statutes, and execute my judgments, and keep all my commandments to walk in them; then will I perform my word with thee, which I spake unto David thy father: And I will dwell among the children of Israel, and will not forsake my people Israel" (1 Kings 6:12–13).

The ark of the covenant would be placed in the temple Solomon was building, and it would be the center of the worship of God's chosen people. God would dwell in the midst of the temple, but only if Solomon keeps God's commandments. Part of these commandments included the construction of the temple itself. Notice some of the commands God gives concerning the interior:

> And within the oracle [sanctuary] he made two cherubims of olive tree, each ten cubits high . . . And he set the cherubims within the inner house . . . And he carved all the walls of the house round about with carved figures of cherubims and palm trees and open flowers, within and without . . . And for the entering of the oracle he made doors of olive tree . . . The two doors also were of olive tree; and he carved upon them carvings of cherubims and palm trees and open flowers [1 Kings 6:23, 27, 29, 31–32].

So God commands Solomon to carve images of things in heaven above and also in the earth beneath. Cherubim, palm trees and open flowers. And notice the cherubim are placed "within the inner house," the inner part of the temple. The most sacred place in all of Israel.

Even more importantly, after the completion of the temple, God declares He is pleased. That's right, God is pleased with Solomon for making graven images for the temple.

> And the Lord said unto him, I have heard thy prayer and thy supplication, that thou hast made before me: I have hallowed this house, which thou hast built, to put my name there for ever; and mine eyes and mine heart shall be there perpetually [1 Kings 9:3].

Now you point out the obvious to Andy and Alice: Their interpretation of Exodus 20:2–5 is clearly mistaken. God is definitely not saying we can't have statues; He's saying we can't worship them. The Catholic Church has always believed this, and has always condemned the worship of anyone or anything other than God.[1]

Alice frowns, "Even if God did command the making of these statues, the Bible doesn't allude to any semblance of the superstitious belief we see in Catholicism. Catholics attribute special powers to statues. They kiss them, kneel before them and believe that they have some magical powers." You explain that the Catholic Church does not believe, nor has ever believed, that any statue or image has any power in and of itself. The beauty of images and icons

---

[1] For a more detailed biblical explanation of the subject of Christians using statues and images for religious purposes, see Patrick Madrid, *Any Friend of God's Is a Friend of Mine* (San Diego: Basilica Press, 1998).

moves us to contemplation of the Word of God as He is Himself or as He works in His saints. They serve to lead us to God, Who is the source of all life and all holiness. They are God's instruments to communicate His life to us.

## Step Two

You show Andy and Alice an example of God using images as His instruments in Numbers 21:8–9:

> And the Lord said unto Moses, "Make thee a fiery serpent, and set it upon a pole: and it shall come to pass, that every one that is bitten, when he looketh upon it, shall live." And Moses made a serpent of brass, and put it upon a pole, and it came to pass, that if a serpent had bitten any man, when he beheld the serpent of brass, he lived.

Our Lord not only commands Moses to make another statue, He commands the children of Israel to look at it in order to be healed. The context of the passage is one where Israel has rebelled against God and a plague of snakes was sent as a punishment and as a general wake-up call to return to the Lord.

The image of the snake Moses constructed had no power in and of itself. We know from John 3:14 it was a type of Christ. The graces the children of Israel received came from Christ in a prevenient sense.

Yet the text is clear. God uses this image of a snake as an instrument to effect healing in His people. The same can be said of statues and icons in Catholic Churches and homes today. They have no power in and of themselves. The images reveal the glory of God in Himself, in His angels and in His saints.

Now you ask Andy and Alice this question: Why would God use these images of serpents, angels, palm trees and open flowers? Further, why not heal the people directly, rather than do so by using a graven image?

The answer is simple, yet profound. God created man as a being who is essentially spiritual and physical. In order to draw us to Himself, God uses both spiritual and physical means. He not only uses spiritual gifts to guide us to our end, but He uses, among other things, statues, the temple, indeed creation itself, to guide us to our ultimate end, which is to be happy with Him for eternity.

Psalm 19:1 tells us, "The heavens declare the glory of God; and the firmament sheweth his handiwork." All of creation is a reflection of God's glory.

Romans 1:20 says, "For the invisible things of him from the creation of the world are clearly seen, being understood by the things that are made, even his eternal power and Godhead; so that they are without excuse." Jesus Himself is "the image (Greek: *icon*) of the invisible God" (Col. 1:15). Before the incarnation, God could not be represented by an image. He was incomprehensible and invisible. But now He has become incarnate, and as such, He has opened up an entirely new economy of images not only of God, but of man as partakers of the divine nature through our union with Him (cf. 2 Peter 1:2–4, 1 John 3:2).

Andy responds, "Second Kings 18:4 tells us, 'He [Hezekiah] removed the high places, and brake the images, and cut down the groves, and brake in pieces the brazen serpent that Moses had made: for unto those days the children of Israel did burn incense to it: and he called it Nehushtan.' When the Israelites began to worship this bronze serpent, God commanded them to destroy it. I have seen Catholics kneel before statues of various saints and even kiss them. This is idolatry, my friend!" You answer, "I believe we're making progress. It sounds to me like you're acknowledging the validity of having statues in churches and homes. What you really abhor is the apparent worship of these statues and images. We Catholics couldn't agree with you more. In fact, the Second Council of Nicea in A.D. 787 officially condemned worshipping anyone or anything other than God. That formal declaration was in response to the heresy of iconoclasm, which erroneously condemned the use of icons, but we Catholics have always worshipped God, and God alone.

But we also believe in honoring God's holy angels and saints. And we believe in honoring statues and icons, inasmuch as they're representations of our Lord, His holy angels and His saints."

## Step Three

Andy has raised two important issues which you now need to address.

First, his use of 2 Kings 18:4. You explain yes, God commanded the destruction of the bronze serpent, but only after it had come to be worshipped; it had been preserved for about 800 years before this. Obviously, God didn't have a problem with this statue being kept around for all those years, then suddenly He had a problem with it. Once again, the problem was not with the statue, but with the worship of it.

His second point: Kneeling before and kissing statues and icons. Just as you begin to answer this question, you realize a few things. 1) You've squeezed every melon in the store at least five times; 2) Your wife is going to wonder what happened to you at the store; and 3) You're about to embark on another topic: the communion of saints.

You politely ask Andy and Alice if you could have their phone number so you could continue this discussion another time. After they oblige, you mention the fact that kneeling before and kissing does not necessarily equal worship. There's an abundance of biblical evidence to support this. For example:

"And he [Jacob] passed over before them, and bowed himself to the ground seven times, until he came near to his brother [Esau] (Gen. 33:3)." "And Bathsheba bowed, and did obeisance unto the king [David] (1 Kings 1:16)." "And the king [Solomon] rose up to meet her [Bathsheba], and bowed himself unto her (1 Kings 2:19)." No one would accuse these of worshipping others as gods.

As far as kissing, St. Paul says four times in Scripture that we're to greet one another with a holy kiss (Rom. 16:16; 1 Cor. 16:20; 2 Cor. 13:12 and 1 Thess. 5:26). And the clergy in Ephesus embrace and kiss St. Paul after his final discourse to them in Acts 20:37.

This is not worship; this is affection. The Bible commands us to "esteem very highly" those who are "over [us] in the Lord" (1 Thess. 5:12–13) and even to give the elders (Greek: *presbyteroi*) "double honor" (1 Tim. 5–17). According to Revelation 5:8, we have elders (Greek: *presbyteroi*) in heaven as well.

Catholics believe, as Scripture makes very clear, that death does not separate us from the love of Christ (cf. Romans 8:38–39) and from His body, which is the Church (Col. 1:24). We may be bodily separated, but this does not keep us from honoring and loving our brothers and sisters and fathers and mothers who have gone before us.

## *Step Four*

Now go on the offensive. Acknowledge the fact that you need more time to fully explain the communion of saints, but remind them how adamant they were about an absolute prohibition against statues and images just a brief time ago. Encourage them to keep an open mind to God's Word, thank them for their time and go call your wife. You need to tell her your grocery shopping took a different turn this week.

# 6

# It's Good to Have
# Friends in High Places

*What the Bible says about asking our departed
brothers and sisters in Christ to pray for us*

## Scenario

It's 7:00 Friday morning. You and your wife are hustling
to perform the daily miracle of getting the kids ready for
school. You've both noticed that one of your boys, Christo-
pher, has not been the energetic, jovial and sometimes mis-
chievous fifteen-year-old you know and love. You ask him
what's wrong. He asks if he could talk to you about it after
you get home from work. Since you both must leave soon,
there's not enough time to explain.

You encourage him not to worry. "Whatever the problem is, Son, it's nothing you and I and our Lord can't handle together." That one gets a little smile out of him, and
you give him a hug as you gather your coat and briefcase
and head for the door. As you kiss your wife good-bye, you
whisper, "We'll get to the bottom of the problem tonight."
Off to work you go.

Upon returning from work at 5:30 and gathering the
troops for dinner, you notice Chris has brought a Bible to
the dinner table. He is quiet throughout supper until finally

he asks, "Can we talk now, Dad?" Your curiosity increases as you lead him into your study and sit him down.

After you convey your concern once again, Chris begins to tell you about an Evangelical in his class at his Catholic school who is challenging everyone concerning their Catholic Faith. Chris had been defending the Faith, but he ran into a few points to which he could not respond. He didn't know what to say, and was afraid to tell you for fear he would disappoint you.

You assure Chris he can always come to you with any problem, and the only way he would disappoint you would be by not coming to you. "So now, Chris, let's get down to business," you say with a smile.

"Well, Dad, he challenged me to prove to him that it's biblical to pray to the saints. He quoted Matthew 6:9 where Jesus commands us to pray to the Father. And in Philippians 4:6, St. Paul tells us to 'let [our] requests be made known to God.' My friend says we're making gods out of the saints. Then he challenged me with Deuteronomy 18:10-11, which condemns necromancing, which is communicating with the dead. That sounds like what we do when we pray to the saints.

"And finally, he told us that Catholics go to the saints as mediators, even though 1 Timothy 2:5 says, 'For there is one God, and there is one mediator between God and men, the man Christ Jesus.' I must admit that the last few days I've been pretty confused about things, Dad."

## Your response

You reassure your son, "First of all, it's not a sin to be confused or have questions about our Faith. But we must remember where to turn when we do have questions. We must always turn to our Lord in prayer and remember: The Church that He built for us has final say in matters of faith and morals. And the Bible teaches this about His Church:

"The apostles in union with St. Peter (and the apostles' successors the bishops, in union with St. Peter's successor the pope) are given authority in Matthew 18:15–18 for just such a situation as this. Scripture says if a dispute cannot be settled among the brethren, the Church makes the final decision on the matter.

"But now we need to respond to the charges made by your friend. First, he seems to be confused about the nature of prayer. Second, about the context of Deuteronomy 18:10 and necromancing. And third, the mediation of Christ as it relates to the mediation of the saints."

## Step One: The Nature of Prayer

You begin by telling your son that when we say we're praying to God and when we say we're praying to the saints, we're talking about two different kinds of prayer. However, we use the same word for both in English.

Prayer to God includes worship that is given to God alone. Prayer to saints includes the honor that is their due, but never worship. The problem is, at least in part, semantics.

Any good dictionary will tell you prayer can simply mean a petition or entreaty from one person to another. That's what we mean by praying to the saints.

Back when people spoke old English, there was no problem. One could say to someone else, "Pray tell" or, "I pray thee, my Lord." In the King James Bible, which was written in old English, we see many examples of this. One is when Bathsheba makes a request of King Solomon in 1 Kings 2:20. She says, "I pray thee, say me not nay." There was never a question as to whether or not Bathsheba was worshipping her son. She wasn't. Nor are Catholics when we pray to saints.

## Step Two: The Accusation of Necromancy

It's true that the verb "necromance" means "to communicate with the dead." It's also true that God condemns this practice in Deuteronomy 18:10–11.

However, the context of the passage makes it very clear: God is condemning communicating with the spiritually dead through wizards and mediums, not condemning praying to saints. This is even more obvious when we see believers praying both for and to those who have "died in the Lord," as well as saints in heaven praying for those on earth in both the Old and New Testaments.

For example, in Jeremiah 31:15–16, we see Rachel interceding for her children (Israel). Jeremiah was written during the time of the Babylonian exile hundreds of years after Rachel's death, yet the text says her "voice [was] heard," and her prayers were answered.

In 2 Maccabees 12:39–45, as Judas Maccabeus is surveying the battlefield the day after Israel had engaged in battle, he and his companions come across the corpses of those who had fallen. Finding amulets under their coats, they surmise the deaths of their comrades to be because of their superstition. So what does Judas Maccabeus do? He takes up a collection to provide a sin offering for the dead and "made atonement for the dead, that they might be delivered from their sin." Though our Protestant friends don't accept the inspiration of 2 Maccabees, you can at least point out it's invaluable for understanding the faith of the Jewish people shortly before the advent of Christ. 2 Maccabees was written around 100 B.C.

This was about the time the sects known as the Pharisees and the Sadducees developed. The Sadducees denied there was a resurrection (Luke 20:27). The author of Maccabees emphasizes what we know is the truth of the resurrection (2 Macc. 12:44). Notice he uses the then common practices of offering sacrifice for the sins of the dead and praying for the dead as his proof that there is a resurrection.

The faith described in Maccabees is the faith in which Jesus was brought up. In Luke 9:28–31, we have proof. Our Lord ascends a mountain with Peter, James and John. There, He is transfigured before them, and Moses and Elijah appeared and "talked with him" about His death (Luke 9:30).

Remember, Chris' friend claimed "communicating with the dead" is condemned. Here our Lord is communicating with the dead. If there's any question as to whether or not Moses did in fact die, check Deuteronomy 34:5. At His transfiguration, Jesus is praying to saints. And aren't Christians supposed to imitate Christ? (cf. 1 Cor. 11:1)

A key to understanding why we can pray to saints is found in Luke 20. Here, Jesus is dealing with the same Sadducees we mentioned before, who denied the resurrection. In verses 28–33, they attempt to trip up our Lord and prove the resurrection to be untenable. They use Deuteronomy 25:5–6 where Moses commands that if a man's brother dies with a wife and no children, he must "raise up seed" for his brother. The Sadducees ask what if seven brothers all marry the same wife? Whose wife will the woman be in the resurrection? Jesus' response is twofold. First, in verse 34 He declares marriage to be only for this world. This is why we believe marriage to be "until death do us part." More important, however, is His second response to the Sadducees.

He says those who die in the Lord "cannot die . . . they are equal to angels. . . . But that the dead are raised, even Moses showed, in the passage about the bush, where he calls the Lord the God of Abraham and the God of Isaac and the God of Jacob. Now he is not God of the dead, but of the living; for all live to him" (Luke 20:36–38).

Jesus uses Moses' words to demonstrate that Abraham, Isaac and Jacob are not dead. They're alive and well in the Spirit. When Catholics pray to saints, we're not praying to the dead (the spiritually dead described in Deut. 18:10–11), but to those who are alive in the Spirit. We use the language "Masses for the dead" and "prayers for the dead," but it's understood we're talking about those who have died in friendship with God.

## Step Three: The Mediatorship of Christ

Finally, you need to straighten out the confusion surrounding 1 Timothy 2:5: "For there is one God, and there is one mediator between God and men, the man Christ Jesus." First, notice the context of 1 Timothy 2:5. In the first two verses, St. Paul commands "supplications, prayers and intercessions to be made for all men." Intercession is a synonym for mediation in the New Testament.

Hebrews 7:25 refers to Jesus as our one unique intercessor. Yet in 1 Tim. 2:5, all Christians are called to be intercessors (or mediators). Notice the first word in verse five: "For there is one God and one mediator." And in verse seven, St. Paul says, "For this I was appointed a preacher and apostle." "Apostle" is another synonym for mediator. The classical definition of an apostle is: "one sent with the authority of the one who sent him." That's also the definition of a mediator.

In short, St. Paul says we are all called to be mediators, for (or because) Christ is the one mediator, and for this reason, St. Paul was called to be a mediator of Christ's love and grace to the world. Does our mediatorship conflict with the mediatorship of Christ? Not at all. Show Chris that the Bible also declares: "But you are not to be called Rabbi, for you have one teacher (Greek: *didaskolos*), and you are all brethren" (Matt. 23:8), yet James 3:1 and Ephesians 4:11 tell us we have many teachers (Greek: *didaskoloi*) in the Church. (Okay, Chris is only 15, but he can handle learning a couple of Greek words once in awhile.)

The key is to understand that the many teachers and mediators in the Body of Christ do not take away from Christ as the one teacher and mediator, they fulfill His command to teach and mediate on this earth in Him. They are, and we are, members of His Body. With St. Paul in Galatians 2:20, we say, "It is no longer I who live, but Christ who lives [or teaches or mediates] in me." Now turn to 1 Corinthians 12:12–27. This is the text that refers to Christians as "the body of Christ." We are so intimately one with one another that in verse 21, the text reads, "The eye cannot say to the hand, 'I have no need of you,' nor again the head to the feet, 'I have no need of you.'" Then add the fact that we are so radically one with Christ that He can say in Matthew 25:40: "Truly, I say to you, as you did it to one of the least of these my brethren, you did it to me." The question is, does this intimate union with Christ and with one another cease when we die? Of course not. In fact, it becomes more radical.

The saints in heaven are even closer to us than when they were here on earth, because it's Christ Who makes us one. They are free from all sin, which hinders our prayers (cf. Matt. 17:20, 1 John 3:22, Psalm 66:18), and they're experiencing a union with God (and therefore with us) beyond anything we can fathom. "[They are] like him for [they] see him as he is" (1 John 3:2). As "partakers of the divine nature" (2 Peter 1:4) in the fullest sense, they have gifts and powers beyond what "eye has seen [or] ear heard" (1 Cor. 2:9). If we could ask them to pray for us when they were here on earth, of course we can — and should — ask them to pray for us now.

And finally, the Bible presents to us a number of good examples of the mediation of the saints in heaven. In the Old Testament, 2 Maccabees 15:12–16 tells of a vision Judas Maccabeus has, in which he sees both Onias (a former high priest who had died) and Jeremiah the prophet (who had died over 500 years earlier) interceding, or mediating, for Israel.

Now turn to Hebrews chapter 12. This chapter is preceded by the great "hall of faith" chapter wherein the lives of the Old Testament saints are recounted. Then, the inspired author encourages a persecuted church (cf. Hebrews 10:32–34) to consider that they are "surrounded by so great a cloud of witnesses" (Heb. 12:1). He then contrasts the Old Testament "church" with the New: "For you have not come to what may be touched, a blazing fire, and darkness, and gloom . . . and the sound of a trumpet, and a voice whose words made the hearers entreat that no further messages be spoken to them" (Heb. 12:18–19).

"But you have come to . . . the city of the living God . . . and to innumerable angels . . . and to the assembly of the first-born who are enrolled in heaven, and to a judge who is God . . . and to the spirits of just men made perfect . . . and to Jesus" (verses 22–24).

Notice the author of Hebrews says, "But you have come to . . . and to . . . and to . . . and to. . . ." In the same way that we come to God and Jesus, we also come to the angels, our brothers and sisters on this earth in the Church, and to the spirits of just men made perfect. Those are the saints in heaven. We come to them all by way of prayer.

The Book of Revelation gives us an even better description of the mediation of both the angels and saints in heaven. In Revelation 5:8, 14, "the twenty-four elders fell down before the Lamb, each holding a harp, and with golden bowls full of incense, which are the prayers of the saints . . . the elders fell down and worshipped." Notice these elders are offering the prayers of the saints. This is the same ministry of mediation we see the angels performing in Revelation 8:3–4 and the martyrs in Revelation 6:10.

Chris is smiling now. As he scribbles the last of the Scripture references in his notebook, he looks as though he'll burst with excitement. "Thanks, Dad. I'm looking forward to Monday morning. It's a bummer I have to wait all weekend before I can use this stuff." As Chris walks out, once more his carefree fifteen-year-old self, you realize you've just experienced a first. It's Friday night during the school year, and your son just wished it were Monday.

As you follow him out to spend the rest of the evening with your family, you marvel at the miracles that never cease, and you ask all the angels and saints to pray for him at school on Monday.

# 7

# I Confess

*What does the Bible say about
confessing your sins to a priest?*

## Scenario

You've decided to help out on a confirmation retreat at
your parish.

You're a small group leader with five candidates in your
group. The youth are responding well until the time comes
to go to confession. One of the girls in your group, Michelle,
has an objection to going to confession.

Her Evangelical boyfriend has apparently convinced her
she has no need of a priest to confess her sins. "Why can't
I confess my sins directly to God?" Michelle protests.

Evidently, Michelle was waiting for this opportunity to
make her stand, because she immediately reels off five
Scripture passages that she had no doubt memorized for
the occasion.

"Isaiah 43:25 says, 'I, even I, am he that blotteth out thy
transgressions for mine own sake, and will not remember thy sins.' It's God who forgives sins," she confidently
proclaims. You notice she is quoting from the King James
Bible.

"Further, Hebrews 3:1 and 7:22–27 tell us Jesus is our

one and only true High Priest and that there are not many priests, but one in the New Testament. The Bible makes it clear in 1 John 2:2 that Jesus 'is the propitiation for our sins,' and not some priest, 'and not for ours only, but also for the sins of the whole world'. And how can we Catholics claim priests act in the role of mediator in confession when 1 Timothy 2:5 tells us, 'For there is one God, and one mediator between God and men, the man Christ Jesus'?"

## *Your response*

You begin by complimenting Michelle on her knowledge of Scripture, and encourage the rest of your group to imitate her in the practice of memorizing Sacred Scripture. You thank her for both her honesty and for bringing up these objections to confession. In answering them, these objections can serve to deepen our understanding of the One, True Faith established by Jesus Christ.

## *Step One*

After thanking Michelle once again for bringing up Isaiah 43:25, which teaches us that it is, in fact, God Who forgives our sins, you ask another member of the group, Mark, to read Leviticus 19:20–22:

> If a man lies carnally with a woman . . . they shall not be put to death . . . but he shall bring a guilt offering for himself to the Lord, to the door of the tent of meeting, a ram for a guilt offering. And the priest shall make atonement for him . . . before the Lord for his sin which he has committed, and the sin which he has committed shall be forgiven him.

Remember, Isaiah 43:25 is an Old Testament passage. It declares that God forgives our sins. On that point all Christians agree. However, here in Leviticus, also in the Old Testament, the priest has been given the ministry of reconciliation. He mediates God's forgiveness to the sinner. Obviously, this does not take away from the fact that it is God Who does the forgiving. God is the efficient, or ultimate, cause of forgiveness. The priest is the instrumental cause.

Michelle immediately objects. "But Jesus is our priest and mediator in the New Testament." You respond, "We'll get to that in a minute, Michelle, but first I want to make sure everyone understands what we're saying." Now, in order to keep this from becoming a confrontation between yourself and Michelle, you turn to the rest of the group and say, "God indeed forgives us our sins, as Isaiah 43:25 teaches. However, that doesn't eliminate the possibility of using priests to mediate that forgiveness to the world as Leviticus 19:20–22 teaches. Right?" You notice Michelle responds affirmatively with the others, so you quickly move ahead.

## Step Two

"Michelle brought up another excellent point we need to address. How can we Catholics have priests to forgive our sins, when Hebrews 3:1 says Jesus is the apostle and High Priest of our confession? And what about Hebrews 7:22–27?" At this point, you ask another member of your small group, Kendra, to read the text.

> This makes Jesus the surety of a better covenant. The former priests were many in number, because they were prevented by death from continuing in office; but he holds his priesthood permanently, because he continues for ever. . . . For it was fitting that we should have such a high priest, holy, blameless, unstained, separated from sinners,

exalted above the heavens. He has no need, like those high priests, to offer sacrifices daily, first for his own sins and then for those of the people; he did this once for all when he offered up himself.

At this point, you see all five of your group members absorbed in thought. Jennifer suddenly pipes up and says, "How do we answer that one? It seems that Jesus is our only priest." To answer, you call on Andrea to read 1 Peter 2:5, 9.

"And like living stones be yourselves built into a spiritual house, to be a holy priesthood, to offer spiritual sacrifices acceptable to God through Jesus Christ . . . But you are a chosen race, a royal priesthood, a holy nation, God's own people. . . ." If Jesus is the one and only priest in the New Testament in the strict sense that Protestants believe, then we have a contradiction in Sacred Scripture, because 1 Peter teaches that all believers are members of a holy priesthood. The key to clearing up this difficulty is in understanding the nature of the Body of Christ. Believers do not take away from Christ's unique Priesthood, rather, as members of His Body, we establish His Priesthood on earth. We are His hands and feet.

Michelle jumps in, "That doesn't say there's any special priesthood we have to go to in order to have our mortal sins forgiven. That text says we're all priests." "We'll get to that," you assure her, "but we are making progress. A moment ago we couldn't see how anyone could be a priest in the New Testament other than Christ, and now we see how all believers are priests.

"Before we move on to demonstrate a special priesthood, can we all see how Christ being the true High Priest does not eliminate the possibility of there being many priests?

We are priests as believers inasmuch as we participate in the one priesthood of Christ, as members of His Body." At this point you clear up the difficulty of 1 Timothy 2:5: "For there is one God, and there is one mediator between God and men, the man Christ Jesus." Yes, Jesus is the one mediator between God and men. However, Christians are also called to be mediators in Him. When we intercede for one another or share the gospel with someone, we act as mediators of God's love and grace in the one true Mediator, Christ Jesus (cf. 1 Tim. 2:1–7, 4:16, Rom. 10:9–14).

Now what about 1 John 2:2? "He is the expiation [propitiation] for our sins, and not for ours only but also for the sins of the whole world." How can we demonstrate from Scripture the existence of a priesthood with the power to forgive sins, within the universal priesthood of all believers?

## Step Three

Now show the context of 1 Peter 2:5, 9. When St. Peter teaches us about the universal priesthood of all believers, he refers to Exodus 19:6 where God speaks of ancient Israel as "a kingdom of priests and a holy nation," a reference to the universal priesthood in the Old Testament "church." But this did not preclude the existence of the Aaronic and Levitical priesthoods within that universal priesthood (cf. Ex. 28 and Num. 3:1–12).

In an analogous way, we have a universal "royal priesthood" in the New Testament, but we also have an ordained clergy who have priestly authority given to them by Christ to carry out His ministry of reconciliation (cf. 2 Cor. 5:17–21, John 20:21–23, James 5:16).

Michelle once again protests: "But you still haven't answered the Scripture I quoted earlier. 1 John 2:2 says Jesus is the propitiation for our sins, not a priest. And in Mark 2:5–10, Jesus forgives the sins of a paralytic. When the scribes object to that and call it blasphemy, Jesus says: ' "But that you may know that the Son of Man has authority to forgive sins on earth," he said to the paralytic, "I say to you, rise, pick up your mat, and go home." ' Scripture is clear. Jesus is the One we go to for forgiveness. Where does the Bible say there's a priesthood with the authority to forgive sins?"

## *Step Four*

Now ask Mark to read John 20:21–23 to the group:

> Jesus said to them again, "Peace be with you. As the Father has sent me, even so I send you." And when he had said this, he breathed on them, and said to them, "Receive the Holy Spirit. If you forgive the sins of any, they are forgiven; if you retain the sins of any, they are retained."

"What does this text say to you?" you ask. Andrea speaks up: "I think it says Jesus gave His authority to forgive sins to His disciples, which we read about in Mark 2." The rest of the group agrees, except for Michelle, who had been listening attentively, but is now studying the text intensely.

You point out the setting: Jesus has risen from the dead and is about to ascend to the Father. In verse 21, Jesus says, "Peace be with you. As the Father has sent me, even so I send you." What did the Father send Jesus to do? He came to be the one true mediator between God and men: proclaiming the gospel (cf. Luke 4:16–21), reigning supreme as King of kings and Lord of lords (cf. Rev. 19:16), and especially, redeeming the world through the forgiveness of sins (cf. 1 Peter 2:21–25, Mark 2:5–10). So this is what Christ is sending the apostles to do in His name: To proclaim the gospel with His authority (cf. Matt. 18:15–17), to govern the Church in His stead (cf. Luke 22:29–30), and to sanctify the Church through the sacraments, especially the Eucharist (cf. John 6:54, 1 Cor. 11:24–29) and confession.

Christ, the High Priest of the New Covenant, ordained the apostles to continue His priestly mission. In John 20:22–23, Jesus then emphasizes this essential part of the priestly ministry of the apostles: forgiving men's sins in the name of Christ. "If you forgive the sins of any, they are forgiven; if you retain the sins of any, they are retained." This is confession. The only way the apostles can either forgive or retain sins is by first hearing those sins confessed, and then making a judgement as to whether or not the penitent should be absolved.

"You mean it's up to the priest to decide whether or not I'm going to be forgiven?" Michelle queries indignantly.

"Yes, Michelle. That's what the Bible teaches here in John 20.

"Let's say a woman confesses adultery," you continue. "When the priest asks her if she's sorry for her sin and resolved to turn away from it, she says she's not. The priest would then be bound to 'retain' her sins. One has to be truly sorry for his or her sins in order to be forgiven." "What if she lies to the priest and says she's sorry when she's not, and then the priest absolves her?" Jennifer asks. "Will she be forgiven?" "No," you respond. "The sacrament does not take effect unless the penitent is truly sorry for his or her sins. In fact, lying in confession is another serious sin, called the sin of sacrilege."

## Step Five

You notice Michelle is much less defensive when she asks her next question. "Do we see any examples of the apostles or church elders actually forgiving sins?" You have Andrea read 2 Corinthians 2:10: "Any one whom you forgive, I also forgive. What I have forgiven, if I have forgiven anything, has been for your sake in the presence of Christ." Actually, a better translation of the phrase "in the presence of Christ" is "in the person of Christ." The Greek word in the passage is *prosopon*. The Latin word *persona* comes from this word. The Greek prefix *pro-* translates to Latin as *per-*. The Greek *sopon* becomes *sona* in Latin. Interestingly, the King James Bible renders the better translation of "person." You read James 5:14–16 aloud:

> Is any among you sick? Let him call for the elders of the church, and let them pray over him, anointing him with oil in the name of the Lord; and the prayer of faith will save the sick man, and the Lord will raise him up; and if he has committed sins, he will be forgiven. Therefore, confess your sins to one another, and pray for one another, that you may be healed. The prayer of a righteous man has great power in its effects.

You point out that Scripture teaches us we must go to the "elders," not just anyone, to receive this "anointing" and the forgiveness of our sins.

Michelle objects. "In verse 16 it says to confess our sins to one another and pray for one another. James is just encouraging us to confess our sins to a close friend so we can help one another to overcome our faults." You respond, "We have to examine the context of Scripture in order to understand it properly. There are two reasons we know St. James is not saying we should confess our sins to just anyone. First, he's just told us to go to the elder, or priest, in verse 14. Then, verse 16 begins with the word "therefore." The word therefore tells us that this statement depends on the verse (or verses) before it — in this case, it connects verse 16 back to verses 14 and 15. It's the elder to whom St. James is telling us to confess our sins.

## Step Six

At this point, there's a break and you decide to take Michelle outside for a little one on one. You ask her, "Well, what do you think?" She replies thoughtfully, "I have to admit that John 20:21–23 and all the rest of the verses you pointed out make it awfully clear. But it's so hard to confess your sins to a man." "I agree," you say. "But I guarantee you, you will walk out of that confessional feeling like you're walking on air. And remember, when the priest says, 'I absolve you of your sins in the name of the Father, and of the Son, and of the Holy Spirit,' there are two people speaking at the same time: the priest, and Jesus Himself, Who loves you more than words could ever say." After the break, it's time for confession. You're watching for Michelle. As soon as she comes out of the confessional, she looks right at you with a bright, beaming smile. As she approaches, you tease, "Was I right?" The smile never leaves her face as she slaps you a high five and walks toward the chapel to pray.

# 8

# Bam! Bam! The "Pebbles" Argument Goes Down

*A bedrock Protestant argument
gets reduced to rubble*

## Scenario

You participate in an employee Bible study every day on your lunch hour. This particular Monday, Fred, a new employee, is introduced to the group. He announces he's a former Catholic and is also a part-time minister at a non-denominational "Bible church" in a nearby town.

As you begin, Fred opens his Bible and begins to "explain" why the papacy is "unbiblical." The other Catholics in the room look to you expectantly. They know you've been attending a Catholic apologetics training course at your parish, and as you look around, you realize you're the only one in the room who is ready to respond.

You take a deep breath and interrupt. "Fred, what exactly is your main objection to the Catholic teaching on the papacy?" Fred's response is as blunt as it is sincere. "It's unbiblical." You grin to hide your nervousness. "Actually, it is biblical, and if you turn to . . ."

"No, it's not."

"Yes, it is." *Man, oh man, this is getting off to a great start*, you think to yourself in exasperation as you open your Bible to Matthew 16:17–19 and read aloud:

> And Jesus answered him, "Blessed are you, Simon Bar-Jona! For flesh and blood has not revealed this to you, but My Father Who is in heaven. And I tell you, you are Peter, and on this rock I will build My Church, and the powers of death shall not prevail against it. I will give you the keys of the kingdom of heaven, and whatever you bind on earth shall be bound in heaven, and whatever you loose on earth shall be loosed in heaven."

"That passage does not refer to Peter as the rock!" Fred emphatically declares. "Contrary to the erroneous Catholic interpretation, it refers to Christ as the rock. For thirty years, I believed that Peter was the rock, but then I found the original Greek proves he wasn't. There's a distinction between the two "rocks" in Greek. The text actually reads, 'You are *petros*,' which means small pebble, 'and on this *petra*,' which means massive boulder, 'I will build My Church.' The first rock is Peter, the second rock is Christ. See? Christ didn't build the Church on Peter, but on Himself."

## Your response

"I understand your argument, but there are problems with it. *Petros* is simply the masculine form of the feminine Greek noun *petra*. Like Spanish and French, Greek nouns have gender. So when the female noun *petra*, large rock, was used as Simon's name, it was rendered in the masculine form as *petros*. Otherwise, calling him *Petra* would have been like calling him Michelle instead of Michael, or Louise instead of Louis." "Wrong." Fred shakes his head.

"*Petros* means a little rock, a pebble. Christ didn't build the Church on a pebble. He is the Rock, the *petra*, the big boulder the Church is built on." You take a deep breath, calm your nerves a little, and continue. "Well, what would you say if I told you that even Protestant Greek scholars like D. A. Carson and Joseph Thayer admit there is no distinction in meaning between *petros* and *petra* in the Koine Greek of the New Testament?[1] As you pointed out, *petra* means a 'rock.' It even usually means a 'large rock.' And that's exactly what *petros* means, too — large rock. It does not mean 'pebble' or 'small stone,' as you've been told. The Greek word for 'pebble' or 'small stone' is *lithos*, not *petros*.

"In Matthew 4:3," you continue, "the devil cajoles Jesus to perform a miracle and transform some stones, *lithoi*, the Greek plural for *lithos*, into bread. In John 10:31, certain Jews pick up stones, *lithoi*, to stone Jesus with. In 1 Peter 2:5, St. Peter describes Christians as 'living stones,' *lithoi*, which form a spiritual house. If St. Matthew had wanted to draw a distinction between a big rock and a little rock in Matthew 16:17–19, he could have by using lithos, but he didn't. The rock is St. Peter!" Wilma, the VP of finance and a member of your parish has a thought, "Fred, how do you explain the fact that Jesus addresses St. Peter directly seven times in this short passage? It doesn't make sense that He would address everything to St. Peter and then say, 'By the way, I'm building the Church on Me.' The context seems pretty clear that Jesus gave authority to St. Peter, naming him the rock." Fred shakes his head. "I

---

[1] Joseph H. Thayer, *Thayer's Greek-English Lexicon of the New Testament* (Peabody: Hendrickson, 1996), 507; D. A. Carson, "Matthew," in Frank E. Gaebelein, ed., *The Expositor's Bible Commentary* (Grand Rapids: Zondervan, 1984), vol. 8, 368.

don't think so. And even if *petros* and *petra* mean the same thing, Jesus surely made the distinction with His hand gestures or tone of voice when He said, 'You are rock, and on this rock I will build My Church.'" Betty, another young Catholic in the group, chimes in. "I don't think it's much use to conjecture about what Jesus' hand gestures or voice intonations might have been, since we can't know what they were. And doesn't that kind of speculation contradict your belief in the 'Bible alone' theory? Anyway, speculation aside, we do know that Jesus definitely said, 'You are rock, and on this rock I will build My Church.' Going from the text alone, His meaning seems crystal-clear to me." You notice several heads nodding in agreement. Fred's isn't one of them. "But getting back to the Greek, Fred," you say, "notice Matthew used the demonstrative pronoun *taute*, which means 'this very,' when he referred to the rock on which the Church would be built: 'You are Peter, and on *taute petra*,' this very rock, 'I will build My Church.'" Also, when a demonstrative pronoun is used with the Greek word for 'and,' which is '*kai*,' the pronoun refers back to the preceding noun. In other words, when Jesus says, 'You are rock, and on this rock I will build My Church,' the second rock He refers to has to be the same rock as the first one. Peter is the rock in both cases.

"Jesus could have gotten around it if He'd wanted to. He didn't have to say, 'And,' *kai*, 'on this rock I will build My Church.' He could've said, 'But,' *alla*, 'on this rock I will build My Church,' meaning another rock. He would have then had to explain who or what this other rock was. But He didn't do that." Fred flips through his Bible. "God says in Isaiah 44:8, 'And you are My witnesses! Is there a God besides Me? There is no Rock; I know not any.' And 1 Corinthians 10:4 says, 'And all drank the same supernatural drink. For they drank from the supernatural Rock which followed them, and the Rock was Christ.' See? These passages tell us Peter could not have been the rock of Matthew 16:17–19. Only God — Christ — is a rock." "That's a good point," you say. "Yes, God is called 'rock' in Isaiah 44:8 and elsewhere. But notice that just seven chapters later in Isaiah 51:1–2, God Himself calls Abraham the rock from which Israel was hewn. Is this a contradiction? No. Jesus is the one foundation of the Church in 1 Corinthians 3:11, but in Revelation 21:14 and Ephesians 2:20, we're told that the Apostles are the foundation of the Church. Jesus said He is the light of the world in John 9:5, but the Bible also says in Matthew 5:14 that Christians are the light of the world. Jesus is our 'one teacher' in Matthew 23:8, yet in Ephesians 4:11 and James 3:1, it says 'there are many teachers' in the Body of Christ.

"Are these contradictions? Of course not. The Apostles can be the foundation of the Church because they are in Christ, the one Foundation. The Church can be the light of the world because she is in the true Light of the world. A teacher can teach because he is in the one true Teacher, Christ. In the same way, St. Peter is indeed the rock of Matthew 16, and that doesn't detract from Christ being the rock of 1 Corinthians 10:4. St. Peter's 'rock-ness' is derived from Christ.

"Aside from everything we said earlier about the Greek," you continue, "there's an even stronger case that can be made for Christ meaning Peter was the rock on which He would build His Church. When Jesus gave Simon the name 'Rock,' we know it was originally given in Aramaic, a sister language of Hebrew, and the language that Jesus and the Apostles spoke. And the Aramaic word for 'rock' is *kepha*. This was transliterated in Greek as *Cephas* or *Kephas*, and translated as *Petros*. In Aramaic, nouns do not have gender as they do in Greek, so Jesus actually said, and St. Matthew first recorded, 'You are *Kephas* and on this *kephas* I will build My Church.' Clearly the same rock both times.

"And just as Greek has a word for 'small stone,' *lithos*, so does Aramaic. That word is *evna*. But Jesus did not change Simon's name to *Evna*, He named him *Kephas*, which translates as *Petros*, and means a large rock." "No way," Fred shakes his head. "There's no evidence in Scripture that Christ spoke in Aramaic or originally gave Simon the name '*Kephas*.' All we have to go on is the Greek, and the Greek says Simon was called *Petros*, a little stone." "Actually, Fred, you're mistaken on both counts. The second point we've already discussed, and as far as your first point, well, take a look at John 1:42. 'Jesus looked at [Simon] and said, "So you are Simon the son of John? You shall be called *Cephas*" (which means Peter).' See? St. John knew that the original form of the name was *Kephas*, large rock, and he translated it into Greek as *Petros*, or Peter." Just then, your watch beeps 1:00, signaling the end of your lunch hour. You close in a quick prayer, then grab a Catholic apologetics tract from inside your Bible and catch Fred on his way out.

"Hey, Fred," you smile warmly. "I really appreciate your input in this group, and I'm glad you've joined us. You're going to add a great new dimension to the group. Welcome!" You extend your hand to shake his.

Fred shakes politely, but you can see on his face that he's not pleased with the way the day's discussion went. But he's a good sport and he promises to be back tomorrow for "round two," as he calls it.

On the way out, you hand him the apologetics tract and smile inwardly at the odd look he gives you as he slips it into his Bible. He's clearly not used to being on the receiving end of a tract, especially not one that's handed to him by a Catholic.

# 9

# Happy Male Parent's Day

*A good son helps clarify what the Son really meant about calling men "father"*

## Scenario

It's Saturday evening. You and a few of your Catholic friends are at a local Fundamentalist church attending a formal debate between a priest, Father Tom Flynn, and the minister, Pastor Doug Simmons. As the evening progresses, you notice Pastor Simmons never refers to Father Flynn as "father," calling him instead, "Mr. Flynn." This strikes you as odd.

At the mid-point of the debate, there's a fifteen-minute break. Hurriedly, you make your way toward Pastor Simmons, where a group is gathering, talking about the first hour. As you approach, you raise your voice above the chatter of the crowd and ask, almost without thinking: "Pastor Simmons? I noticed you never refer to Father Flynn as 'father.' Can you give me a reason why?" The crowd quiets a little as he immediately responds, "Certainly. Matthew 23:9 tells us quite clearly, 'Call no man your father on earth, for you have one Father, who is in heaven.' I obey Jesus Christ, rather than the false doctrines and precepts of men."

## *Your response*

Though you feel a bit nervous to find yourself engaged in an impromptu debate with an experienced debater, you ask, "What if I can demonstrate to you from the Bible that it is entirely proper to call men 'father' on the earth? Would you then call Father Flynn 'father' for the rest of the debate?" "Sure," Pastor Simmons confidently responds.

"Good luck trying," you overhear one bystander say to another.

## *Step One*

"I think we all agree we must never take Scripture out of context," you begin. "Jehovah's Witnesses are a classic example of this. They will quote 1 Timothy 2:5 as proof against the Divinity of Christ: 'For there is one God; and there is one mediator between God and men, the man Christ Jesus.' They claim this text proves Jesus is not God. We all know, as Christians, this is not the case (John 1:1, 8:58, 20:28, Hebrews 1:8, Titus 2:13). We must be sure never to build a doctrine on one single verse, without acknowledging its context or other Biblical evidence. And I hate to say it, Pastor Simmons, but I believe this is what you're doing with Matthew 23:9."

## *Step Two*

Now you ask them to turn in their Bibles to Ephesians 6:2–4: " 'Honor your father and mother, that it may be well with you and that you may live long on the earth. Fathers, do not provoke your children to anger, but bring them up in the discipline and instruction of the Lord.' Wouldn't you say your father is someone on this earth? But Jesus said 'call no man your father on earth.' Jesus did not say 'call no man father on earth except your biological father.' Is this a contradiction?" you ask.

"Of course not," Pastor Simmons responds. "As you said, we must consider the context of any given passage of Scripture. Clearly, in Matthew 23, Jesus is speaking in the context of calling religious leaders 'father.'" You reply, "So you're saying that when Jesus said 'call no man your father on earth,' He didn't mean that in an absolute and all-encompassing way? We have an exception when it comes to our biological fathers. Is that correct?" "That is correct," Pastor Simmons declares assuredly. "We just can't refer to religious leaders as 'fathers.'"

## Step Three

Now you step up the challenge. "What if I can show you that it is Biblical to call religious leaders 'father'? Would you then call Father Flynn 'father'?" "Absolutely," Pastor Simmons grins.

"Then listen to the very words of Our Lord in Luke 16:24: 'And he [the rich man] called out, Father Abraham, have mercy upon me, and send Lazarus to dip the end of his finger in water and cool my tongue; for I am in anguish in this flame.' Would you say Abraham is a religious leader, Pastor?" Silence.

You continue: "Not only does Jesus refer to Abraham as 'father,' but St. James does likewise in James 2:21, as does St. Paul, calling Abraham 'father' seven times in Romans 4:1–18. Are we to believe Jesus, St. James and St. Paul are contradicting Matthew 23:9?" At this point, Pastor Simmons is visibly frustrated as he responds, "It's okay to refer to someone who has gone before us in the faith as 'father.' They are our 'fathers' in the faith. But this is a far cry from giving our leaders today the title of 'father,' which, according to Matthew 23:9, is reserved to God alone."

## Step Four

As the surrounding crowd listens intently, you summarize the mini-debate thus far. "What began as a Scripture text 'clearly' prohibiting calling any man 'father' has now become a text with two exceptions so far. So now you're saying it's okay to call our dads 'father.' We can even call our spiritual forefathers 'father,' as we see with Abraham in Scripture. But you still claim we cannot refer to our living spiritual leaders as 'father.' What if I can demonstrate to you it is in fact Biblical to call our living spiritual leaders 'father'? Would you then refer to Father Flynn as 'father'?" Receiving no response this time, and seeing you are quickly running out of time, you proceed. "Twice in 1 John 2:13–14, St. John calls the leaders of the Church to which he is writing 'fathers':

> I am writing to you, fathers, because you know him who is from the beginning. I am writing to you, young men, because you have overcome the evil one. I write to you, children, because you know the Father. I write to you, fathers, because you know him who is from the beginning?

In Acts 7:1–2, St. Stephen, under the inspiration of the Holy Spirit as shown in Acts 7:55, calls both Abraham and the elders of Jerusalem 'father': 'And the high priest said, "Is this so?" And Stephen said: "Brethren and fathers, hear me. The God of glory appeared to our father Abraham."'

And in 1 Corinthians 4:14–15, St. Paul refers to himself as 'father':

> I do not write this to make you ashamed, but to admonish you as my beloved children. For though you have countless guides in Christ, you do not have many fathers. For I became your father in Christ Jesus through the gospel.

Time does not allow me to quote to you 1 Thessalonians 2:11, John 4:12, Acts 4:25 and Romans 9:10. All of these verses refer to men, whether alive at the time or not, as being called 'father.'"

## Step Five

Now you're almost out of time, so you rush to make your final points quickly. "In Matthew 23:8, one verse earlier than the text in question, it says to call no man 'teacher.' And yet, we know there are many who are called 'teacher' in the New Testament, for instance in James 3:1 and Ephesians 4:11.

"The real key to understanding Matthew 23," you explain, "is found in a proper understanding of the nature of the Body of Christ. The Douay-Rheims translation of Ephesians 3:14–15 expresses it well. 'For this cause I bow my knees to the Father of our Lord Jesus Christ, of whom all paternity [Greek: *paternia*, English: fatherhood] in heaven and earth is named.' God the Father is our one, true Father. All other fatherhood, be it biological or spiritual, participates in His unique Fatherhood and represents it to us. Our biological and spiritual fathers neither take away nor add to this one unique Fatherhood. Rather, they establish it on earth.

"The context of Matthew 23 shows that it's addressing the sin of pride among the scribes and Pharisees. They loved to be called 'teacher' and 'father.' But in their pride, they pointed to themselves rather than to God the Father, from Whom they received true fatherhood, and in Whom their fatherhood subsisted. Outside of God the Father, there are no fathers at all in the true sense of the term.'"

## Conclusion

The moderator of the debate now summons the audience back to their seats for the second half. As the small crowd disperses, you remind Pastor Simmons to remember what Scripture says about the nature of Christ. "There are texts that say Christ is man and there are texts that say He is God. We don't throw out either. Both are true. Analogously, Jesus says we are not to call any man 'father,' yet Christ Himself, St. Stephen, St. James and St. Paul all refer to men as 'father.'" Your final comment to him is this: "Don't throw out any of these texts! Our fathers in heaven, Abraham, David and Jacob for example, and our fathers on earth, religious leaders and dads, participate in the one, unique Fatherhood of God. They don't add to it, but neither do they detract from it. They represent and establish that Fatherhood on earth." As the debate resumes, you notice a significant change. Pastor Simmons is not quite the man he was before the break. Several times, when referring to Father Flynn by name, he hesitates in calling him "Mister." It's obvious the wheels are turning in his head.

You sit back in your chair, and can't help smiling to yourself. "Here I am," you think, "an average Catholic just dabbling in apologetics, yet the Lord used me to help a Protestant minister and some of his flock rethink what once seemed so certain. I can't wait to call Dad and tell him all about it."

# 10

# Batting Around the Great Apostasy

*Having a ball with some Mormon elders*

## Scenario

It's a scorching hot Saturday afternoon in early September. Your wife has taken the little ones to the pool. It's just you and your oldest, ten-year-old Matthew, staying in to watch the big game. Mark McGwire has now hit 59 home runs! And the way he's been connecting, he could catch Roger Maris' thirty-seven-year-old record of 61 homers in today's game. Your son is decked out in his "McGwire" jersey and you've just poured ice-cold drinks for the start of the game when the doorbell rings. You hurry to the door, thinking of ways to get rid of whoever it is as quickly as possible. Opening it, however, you discover two sweat-drenched young men wearing white shirts and ties. With beaming smiles, they introduce themselves as Elders Joseph McCarthy and Leonard Smith. "We're from the Church of Jesus Christ of Latter-day Saints. We'd like to offer you some free literature and talk to you about the Lord and Savior Jesus Christ."

## Your Response

For a moment you freeze, thinking to yourself, "Why now, Lord? What about the game?" Quickly, you come to your senses. "Which is more important, Maris' record being broken or the salvation of two immortal souls?" So you invite them in. As you ask them to be seated in the living room where your son is engrossed in the game, you wonder if he'll see things the way you do.

Matthew winces a bit when you tell him you must turn the game off while you talk with these young Mormons. You're delighted, however, when his disappointment changes to excitement. (All that home schooling is paying off.) Matthew wants to talk about the Faith!

## Step One

Rather than wait for their scripted presentation, you decide to cut to the chase and begin the dialogue. You start by complimenting the Mormon Church on its belief in an authoritative, hierarchical church. You comment that of all the sects that have begun in the last 480 years, only theirs even *claims* to have apostolic authority. According to Ephesians 4:11–15, St. Paul tells us the true Church of Jesus Christ must have *"apostles*, some prophets, some evangelists, some pastors and teachers . . ." This leads you to the big question. "Why would I ever leave the Catholic Church which was founded by Jesus Christ and received apostolic authority directly from Him and the Apostles? This is so clearly attested to by both Scripture and many early Christian writers like St. Clement of Rome (A.D. 90), St. Ignatius of Antioch (A.D. 107), St. Irenaeus of Lyons

(A.D. 180), St. Hippolytus (A.D. 200), St. Cyprian (A.D. 250), Eusebius of Caesarea (A.D. 330), St. Ambrose (A.D. 390), St. Augustine (A.D. 410), St. Jerome (A.D. 410), etc. The bishops in the Catholic Church are the successors of the Apostles and have true apostolic authority."

Elder Smith responds, "We believe the Church Jesus established fell into apostasy after the death of the last Apostle, as was foretold in the Bible in both Amos 8:11–14 and 2 Thessalonians 2:1–4. It has been re-established through another Testament given to Joseph Smith and the Church of Jesus Christ of Latter-day Saints."

## Step Two

You respond with a challenge. "Let's get out a Bible and look at those two texts you just mentioned. We'll begin with Amos. Amos prophesied around 780 B.C. Among other things, he warned of the coming destruction of Israel that would, in fact, occur in 721 B.C. (because of her idolatry — cf. chapters six and seven)." The passage Elder Smith cited reads:

> "Behold, the days are coming," says the Lord God, "when I will send a famine on the land; not a famine of bread, nor a thirst for water, but of hearing the words of the Lord. They shall wander from sea to sea, and from north to east; they shall run to and fro, to seek the word of the Lord, but they shall not find it . . . ."

"This text speaks of an apostasy in ancient Israel, not after the death of the last apostle in New Testament times. But even this apostasy was not total. In the very next chapter (9:8–10), Amos makes this very clear:

"Behold, the eyes of the Lord God are upon the sinful kingdom, and I will destroy it from the surface of the ground; except that *I will not utterly destroy the house of Jacob*," says the Lord. "For lo, I will command, and shake the house of Israel among all the nations as one shakes with a sieve, but no pebble shall fall upon the earth. *All the sinners of my people shall die by the sword, who say, 'Evil shall not overtake or meet us.'*"

"There were many incidents in Old Testament salvation history when priests and prophets were corrupt (Lam. 4:13, Ezek. 22:22–26, Zeph. 1:4, Mic. 3:5), prophets had no vision from the Lord, prophesied falsely (Lam. 2:14, Jer. 23:26–31), or at times, there were no prophets at all (Ps. 74:9). Apostasies were frequent in the Old Testament, but *never total*. There was always a faithful remnant."

## Step Three

Now you move to a crucial point concerning Old Testament hierarchy. In the midst of good times and bad, there was one constant in all of Old Covenant salvation history: the existence of the High Priesthood and the Levitical Priesthood as they are detailed in Exodus 28 and Deuteronomy 17. God established and gave authority to them to guide the children of Israel. The High Priest, or those to whom the High Priest delegated authority, had the power to deliver the oracle of God to His people.

Deuteronomy 17:8–12 is an example of this historical fact:

If any case arises requiring decision between one kind of homicide and another, one kind of legal right and another, or one kind of assault and another, any case . . . which is too difficult for you, then you shall . . . go up to . . . the

Levitical priests, and to the judge who is in office in those days, you shall consult them, and they shall declare to you the decision. Then you shall do according to what they declare . . . you shall be careful to do according to all that they direct you. . . . The man who acts presumptuously, by not obeying the priest who stands to minister there before the Lord your God, or the judge . . . shall die.

According to Exodus 28:30, the High Priest had what was called the "Urim and the Thummim" on the breastplate of his vestments whereby he would bear the sins of the people of Israel when he went before the Lord in the temple. Through this gift of God, the High Priest would also hear the Word of God and proclaim divine oracles from God.

Even during such a corrupt time as the time of the Judges, we see this gift in operation in Israel. This was a time when "every man did what was right in his own eyes" (Judges 17:6). Yet, even then, this gift of "the Urim and the Thummim" was alive and well. And when the Israelites consulted God through "Phineas the son of Eleazar the son of Aaron," who was High Priest at the time (cf. Judges 20:18–28), they received the oracle of God through him. They may not have always consulted the Lord or obeyed Him, but He was always there for them.

In fact, our Lord Jesus Christ Himself acknowledges the existence of this hierarchy and its authority in His time. In Matthew 23:2–3, Jesus says to his disciples, "The scribes and Pharisees *sit on Moses' seat;* so practice and observe whatever they tell you, but not what they do; for they preach, but do not practice." Even the Apostles must obey the scribes and Pharisees who speak in an official capacity with delegated authority from the High Priest. Note: they

must do so even if the legitimate authority may be personally corrupt (see also John 11:47–52).

Elder Smith responds, "Even if the Old Testament people of God never completely apostatized, St. Paul prophesied the New Covenant people of God would in 2 Thessalonians 2:1–4. He even used the word *apostasia* in verse
3 to describe it. He declared this apostasy must occur before Jesus would come again. And after all, didn't the Jews
themselves reject the Messiah and apostatize? Doesn't this
at least demonstrate that an apostasy is possible?"

## *Step Four*

You respond, "First of all, not all of Israel apostatized.
The Apostles, Mary and the earliest disciples were mostly
Jews! And remember, the Church is 'the Israel of God'
(Gal. 6:16). And 'he is not a real Jew who is one outwardly,
nor is true circumcision something external and physical.
He is a Jew who is one inwardly, and real circumcision is
a matter of the heart . . .' (Rom. 2:28). St. Paul describes
the relationship between Jews and Christians in Romans
11:18–29, but once again, I emphasize the fact that a total
apostasy simply did not occur. There isn't one shred of biblical evidence that says otherwise. And to put it frankly, a
total apostasy, as you describe it, is impossible in the New
Testament. There are three reasons for this:

"First, the Old Testament prophecies concerning the
New Covenant describe it as perpetual and indefectible.
For example, Daniel 7:13–14:

> I saw in the night visions, and behold, with the clouds
> of heaven there came one like a son of man [Jesus], and
> he came to the Ancient of Days and was presented be-

fore him. And to him was given dominion and glory and kingdom, that all peoples, nations, and languages should serve him; his dominion is an everlasting dominion, which shall not pass away, and *his kingdom one that shall not be destroyed* [cf. Isaiah 9:6–7 and Daniel 2:44].

"Second, the New Testament also describes the Church as indefectible. Yes, there will be apostasies. That is what St. Paul is referring to in 2 Thessalonians. In fact, there will be a major apostasy before the Second Coming according to 2 Thessalonians 2, but never does it say a total apostasy. According to the New Testament, this is impossible! Matt. 28:19–20 says,

> And Jesus came and said to them, "All authority in heaven and on earth has been given to me. Go therefore and make disciples of all nations, baptizing them in the name of the Father and of the Son and of the Holy Spirit, teaching them to observe all that I have commanded you; and lo, *I am with you always, to the close of the age.*"

A similar thought can be found in Luke 1:33, where the Angel Gabriel says of Jesus, 'And of his kingdom there will be no end.'"

Just as you finish quoting this last verse, your son says, "Daddy, what about when Jesus gave the keys of the kingdom to St. Peter? Didn't Jesus say the gates of hell would never overcome the Church?" (Cf. Matt. 16:15–19) You feel so proud, you want to jump through the roof. "Yes, son, that's an excellent point!"

Elder Joseph then responds, "Those verses merely speak of the ultimate triumph of the Church. We agree with that. But that doesn't mean there would not be an apostasy in the centuries between the time of the Apostles and now."

"I'm glad you bring that up, because that leads me to the third reason why a total apostasy is impossible," you retort. "Matthew 28:20 says the Lord will be with us, *pasas tas hemaras*, or 'all the days'! So there's no room for total apostasy. Christ will be teaching via his apostles and their successors *all days even until the end of time!*

"In Ephesians, St. Paul explicitly tells us the Church will be with us until the end of time. Ephesians 1:22 describes the Church as '[Christ's] body, the *fullness of him who fills all in all*.' This Church is 'built upon the apostles and prophets, Christ Jesus himself being the chief cornerstone' (2:20). She is described as being so awesome, St. Paul can say 'through the Church the manifold wisdom of God might now be made known to the principalities and powers in heavenly places' (3:10). The Church teaches angels!

"As we saw before, this true Church must have apostles, prophets, pastors, evangelists and teachers (cf. 4:11). And why, you ask? 'For the equipment of the saints . . . for building up the body of Christ . . . so that we may no longer be children, tossed to and fro and carried about with every wind of doctrine . . .' (4:12, 14).

"So, God gave us the Church that we may know with certainty the truths of the Faith. That's not the only reason, but it is a central reason. But maybe the most important passage for us in Ephesians is 3:20–21:

'Now to him who by the power at work within us is able to do far more abundantly than all that we ask or think, to him be glory *in the Church* and in Christ Jesus *to all generations, forever and ever. Amen*.'

"This Church that St. Paul is describing in Ephesians will be here to *all generations* (*pasas tas geneas*, 'all the generations') *forever and ever*. This eliminates the possibility of a total apostasy for even one generation!"

At this point, Elder Smith says it's time for them to get going, but that they'd like to come back with someone who would be better able to respond to what you're saying. You realize you may well be making progress, so you agree and you give them one last thing to think about. As you all say your good-byes, you ask them this question:

"According to Matthew 18:15–18, Jesus gives us a commandment. He says if we have a difficulty with a brother, we try and settle the difficulty with him personally. If we can't settle it, we take two or three with us and try to work it out then. Let's say the difficulty we have with our brother is over the nature of God. The question is whether or not God is a Trinity. If we still cannot settle the difficulty, we 'tell it to the Church.' If he fails to listen to the Church, he is to be excommunicated. The question is, what Church is being referred to here?"

Elder Smith responds without pause, "Jesus is talking about the true Church, which I testify to you is the Church of Jesus Christ of Latter-day Saints."

You answer, "But what if you're living in 1785, and you have this same difficulty? In obedience to Jesus, where do you go then? Your church doesn't exist yet."

There is silence. After an awkward moment, you calmly say, "Fellas, Jesus is the way, the truth and the life. He would never lead us astray or command us to follow error. If the true Church didn't exist on this earth for 1,700 years, then Jesus misguided millions into obeying error-filled churches with no apostolic authority. And that's ridiculous."

As you shake hands, you invite them to return anytime. Then, as they turn to leave, little Matthew says, "I hope you guys become Catholic — that would be really cool." Matthew closes the door. Looking at him with pride you say, "Yeah, that *would* be really cool. Now, let's go see what McGwire did!"

# 11

# We Are Here
# To Pump You Up

*Working out the Divinity of the Holy Spirit,
and other weighty matters*

## Scenario

It's Monday morning. You're at the gym working out
when in walks Charles, a Jehovah's Witness. He's often at
the gym at the same time you are, and you've had a couple of lively discussions about the divinity of Christ. After
a few minutes of small talk, you pick up the argument
where you last left off. In between sets of biceps curls and
triceps pushdowns, you assert Christ is *clearly* referred to
as God throughout the New Testament (John 1:1–3, 5:17–
18, 8:58, 20:28, Acts 20:28, Philippians 2:5, Colossians 2:9,
Titus 2:13, Hebrews 1:8–10, etc.).

In the middle of the discussion, another iron-pumping
patron named Steve gets into the fray. You're relieved to
discover he's on your side. Not only is it nice to have someone to help you, but from the looks of him, he's not the
kind of guy you want to make angry. Paint him green and
you've got the Incredible Hulk.

Things are going great and it seems as though you and
the Hulk are getting through to Charles, when the topic

of discussion moves to the divinity of the Holy Spirit. It's then you discover that Steve is a member of a group that espouses the doctrine of the late Herbert W. Armstrong (founder of the World-Wide Church of God). They believe the Father and the Son are God, but the Holy Spirit is not.

When you mention the fact that the current leadership of the World-Wide Church of God has acknowledged the truth about the Trinity, Steve calls them apostates. You realize it's now going to be two against one with you being the "one" defending the divinity of the Holy Spirit!

## Point One

Steve notes that the Greek word for "spirit" (*pneuma*) is neuter. He points to John 14:26 which refers to the Spirit as *to pneuma to hagion* (Holy Spirit), and is indeed neuter. "The *Father* and the *Son* are clearly personal, masculine terms. There's no doubt we're dealing with persons who are masculine," he says, hefting a bar-full of weights. "But 'spirit,' being neuter, indicates we're dealing with an impersonal force rather than a person." Charles agrees as they both look to you for a response.

## Your Response

While you agree with the fact that "spirit" in Greek is a neuter term, this doesn't necessarily mean the Holy Spirit is impersonal. Nouns in Greek are assigned gender as they are in many languages. In Latin and the modern romance languages, this is the case as well. For example, the Latin word for "lance" is *lancea*, which is feminine. This doesn't mean that lances or daggers are actually female and personal! The same can be said for Greek words like *kardia*, which means, "heart." The fact that this Greek word is feminine doesn't indicate that hearts are female. Nor does the fact that *baros*, Greek for "arrow," which is neuter, indicate arrows to be impersonal forces. Words are simply assigned gender in these languages.

Further, if being referred to as "spirit" means the third person of the Blessed Trinity is impersonal, then both angels and God the Father would have to be "forces" rather than persons as well. In John 4:24, Jesus says, "God is spirit [*pneuma*] and those who worship him must worship in spirit and truth." And in Hebrews 1:14, angels are referred to as "ministering spirits [*pneumata*] sent forth to serve, for the sake of those who are to obtain salvation."

Most importantly, the very verse Steve used (John 14:26) to "prove" the Spirit is an impersonal force actually demonstrates the Holy Spirit to be both personal and masculine. It says: "But *the Counselor*, the Holy Spirit, whom the Father will send in my name, *He* will *teach* you all things, and *bring to your remembrance* all that I have said to you."

There are three key points to be made here. First, "the Counselor" (*ho paracleto*) in Greek is masculine, not neuter. Second, when the text says *He* will teach you all things, the demonstrative pronoun (*ekeinos*) is used in the masculine singular. This is very significant because the inspired author could have used the neuter *ekeino*; he did not. If the Holy Spirit were an impersonal force, John would not refer to "it" as a "He." Third, notice what the Holy Spirit *does*. Jesus says He will both *teach* and *remind* us "all that [He has] said to [us]." Action follows being. One cannot teach and remind if one doesn't have the intellectual powers unique to rational beings! The Holy Spirit is clearly personal.

As you finish your point, you notice Steve nodding in

agreement. Maybe you're making an impact! Now you pour it on by showing him and Charles just how often the Holy Spirit is referred to in personal terms. To keep it manageable, you restrict yourself to John chapters 14, 15 and 16. In John 14:16–17, Jesus says, "And I will pray the Father, and He will give you another Counselor, to be with you for ever, even the Spirit of truth, who the world cannot receive, because it neither sees *Him* nor knows *Him*; you know *Him*, for *He* dwells with you, and will be in you."

In John 14:26, Jesus says, "But the Counselor, the Holy Spirit, Whom the Father will send in My name, *He* will teach you all things, and *bring to your remembrance* all that I have said to you."

In John 15:26, Jesus says, "But when the Counselor comes, Whom I shall send to you from the Father, even the Spirit of Truth, who proceeds from the Father, *He* will bear witness to me; and you also are witnesses, because you have been with Me from the beginning."

Finally, in John 16:7–13, Jesus makes it very plain:

> Nevertheless I tell you the truth: it is to your advantage that I go away, for if I do not go away, the Counselor will not come to you; but if I go, I will send *Him* to you. And when *He* comes, *He* will convince the world of sin and of righteousness and of judgment: of sin, because they do not believe in Me; of righteousness, because I go to the Father, and you will see Me no more; of judgment, because the ruler of this world is judged. I have yet many things to say to you, but you cannot bear them now. When the Spirit of truth comes, *He* will guide you into all the truth; for *He* will not speak on *His* own authority, but whatever *He* hears *He* will speak, and *He* will declare to you *the things that are to come. He* will glorify me, for *He* will take what is mine and declare it to you. All that the Father has is

mine; therefore I said that *He* will take what is mine and declare it to you.

The Holy Spirit is clearly personal. He convinces of sin, teaches the truth, speaks, declares things that are to come, etc. There is no doubt as to the person of the Holy Spirit in these texts.

Next, you point out that the passage says the Holy Spirit "guides [us] into all truth." In fact, in 1 Corinthians 2:11, the Scripture indicates the Holy Spirit is omniscient: "For what person knows a man's thoughts except the spirit of the man which is in him? So also no one comprehends the thoughts of God except the Spirit of God." Only the Spirit of God fully comprehends the thoughts of God because He *is* God.

## Point Two

While Steve appears convinced, Charles does not. Taking your Bible (which you *always* bring to the gym), he reads Acts 2:17 which quotes Joel 2:28: "I will *pour out* my spirit upon all flesh . . ." "How can you 'pour out' a person?" Charles asks. "Isn't this clear proof the Holy Spirit is a force rather than a person?"

## Your Response

You refer Charles to Psalm 22:15. This is a messianic Psalm referring to Christ's passion. Notice how it describes our Lord: "I am poured out like water . . ." Would we say Jesus is just a force and not a person because He is "poured out" in this verse? Of course not! So it goes with the Holy Spirit. Catholics don't deny the plain verses of Scripture indicating the Spirit's personhood just because He's also described as being "poured out" in Acts 2:17.

You've been saving the best for last. Just before it's time to leave, you point Charles to Hebrews 3:7–10 and Hebrews 10:15–17 for some very plain biblical references to the divinity of the Holy Spirit. Hebrews 3:7–10 reads:

> Therefore, as *the Holy Spirit says*, "Today, when you hear His voice, do not harden your hearts as in the rebellion, on the day of testing in the wilderness, where your fathers put *Me* to the test and saw *My* works for forty years. Therefore *I* was provoked with that generation, and said, 'They always go astray in their hearts; they have not known *My* ways.' . . ."

Notice that the Holy Spirit is synonymous with God Himself. In Hebrews 10:15–17, the reference is even more plain and unmistakable:

> And *the Holy Spirit also bears witness to us*; for after saying, "This is the covenant that *I* will make with them after those days, *says the Lord: I* will put *My* laws on their hearts, and write them on their minds," then *He* adds, "*I* will remember their sins and their misdeeds no more."

The passage is clear: the Holy Spirit is both divine and a person. He is clearly depicted as "bear[ing] witness," "establish[ing] a covenant," is referred to as "the Lord," "puts [His] laws on [our] hearts" and even forgives sins. You see you've gotten through to Steve, but Charles seems to have more questions. Giving them each a pamphlet on the Blessed Trinity, you agree to meet again in a couple of days.

"Not a bad day at the gym," you think to yourself. "I saw a Jehovah's Witness come to see the truth about the divinity of Christ and a member of the World-Wide Church of

God come to see the divinity of the Holy Spirit. They still have questions about the Catholic Faith, but are definitely off to a great start! And I got a pretty good biceps/triceps workout as well. Not a bad day's work."

# 12

# Justification, Works and Doughnuts

*Apologetics over snacks*

## Scenario

You and several close friends are talking after Sunday Mass at the parish "coffee and doughnut fellowship." Your pastor has just given a rousing homily wherein he spoke of the obligation we have to share our faith with others in both word and deed. In particular, he mentioned how the Holy Father has challenged all of us to share the One, Holy, Catholic and Apostolic Faith with those "sects" that have been leading many Catholics astray over the last several decades.

Father made one point that especially caught your attention. He noted how he's encountered an alarming number of Catholics who have been influenced by Protestant television and radio ministries and don't realize it. He finds Catholic parishioners saying things contrary to the Faith without even knowing they're contrary to the teachings of the Church.

Just as you're about to compliment your pastor's sermon, another parishioner, Martin, interrupts and expresses his disapproval. "I think Father's homily was out of order," he says insistently. "I watch Protestant Christian television all the time and I benefit greatly from it, but I'm still Catholic. It hasn't affected me in a negative way."

You respond by encouraging Martin to *at least* consider the things Father had said. "Father McDuff is a very wise and knowledgeable man when it comes to the Faith. One of the examples Father mentioned was justification. James 2:24 *clearly* tells us that we're justified 'not by faith alone.' Yet, as Father said, some Catholics deny the necessity of good works in the Christian life. This is, no doubt, an example of the influence of the notion of 'justification by faith alone' popular in Protestant ministries."

Just as you make this statement, Martin again jumps in. "Why is Father so hung up on all of these doctrines? What's most important is believing in Jesus, isn't it? And why are we even talking about evangelizing people who already believe in Jesus anyway? After all, the Bible *does say* we are saved by our faith in Christ and not by works. If we're going to evangelize, we should be evangelizing the unchurched. You people are obsessed with works and are missing what is most essential about the Faith."

## Your Response

"I hate to tell you, Martin, but what you just said is *precisely* an example of what Father McDuff was talking about. You said that works have nothing to do with our salvation — only faith. That's contrary to the teaching of the Catholic Church!"

You then point out to Martin that his misconception is rooted in the same false interpretation of Romans 3:28 and

Romans 4:5 commonly presented on Protestant Christian television and radio programs. Romans 3:28 says, "For we hold that a man is justified by faith apart from works of law." And Romans 4:5 says, "And to one who does not work but trusts him who justifies the ungodly, his faith is reckoned as righteousness." It sounds on the surface like St. Paul is saying works aren't necessary for our justification. However, that's not the case when we examine the *context* of these passages.

## *Step One*

You first point out to Martin what St. Paul has already made very clear in Romans 2:6–11. Good works *are necessary for eternal life*:

> For he will render to every man *according to his works*: to those who by *patience in well-doing* seek for glory and honor and immortality, *he will give eternal life*; but for those who are factious and *do not obey the truth*, but obey wickedness, there will be wrath and fury. There will be tribulation and distress for every human being who *does evil*, the Jew first and also the Greek, but glory and honor and peace for every one who *does good*, the Jew first and also the Greek. For God shows no partiality.

The context of Paul's Epistle to the Romans clears up the misunderstanding. One of the problems in Rome with which St. Paul was dealing was a very prominent heresy of the first century known as the Judaizer heresy. This sect taught that belief in Christ and obedience to the New Covenant wasn't enough to be saved. One had to keep the Levitical law (which, according to Hebrews 7:11–12, has passed away in Christ) and be circumcised (see also Acts 15:1–2). It's obvious St. Paul has this sect in mind when he says in Romans 2:28–29, "For he is not a real Jew who is one outwardly, nor is *true circumcision* something external and physical. He is a Jew who is one inwardly, and *real circumcision* is a matter of the heart, spiritual and not literal . . ." This same St. Paul tells us that the true "circumcision of Christ" is New Covenant *baptism* in Colossians 2:11–12.

It's in this context that St. Paul says we are "justified by faith *apart from the works of the law*." He didn't say that no works are required in any sense. He specified the *works of the law* because these were the very works without which the Judaizers were claiming one "cannot be saved" (cf. Acts 15:1–2).

At this point, Martin responds, "But St. Paul doesn't say 'works of the law' in Romans 4:5. And what do you do with Romans 7:7, where St. Paul uses the ninth and tenth commandments as his example of 'the law' in his discourse? This isn't the Levitical law that has passed away; this is talking about the Ten Commandments!"

You're happy to hear Martin is still Catholic enough to know when St. Paul mentions "thou shall not covet" in Romans 7:7, he's talking about the ninth *and* tenth commandments, rather than just the tenth! But you also realize someone has seriously misled Martin about the nature of "works" in Sacred Scripture. It's time to do some heavy apologetics!

## Step Two

You tell Martin that he's correct — St. Paul doesn't say works *of the law* in Romans 4:5. But the *context* makes it very clear that St. Paul is referring to circumcision in particular (and to the same "works of the law" to which he was referring in Romans 3:28). Just check out verses 5–16. When it comes to Romans 7:7, St. Paul uses the ninth and tenth commandments as examples of "the law." But, St. Paul is using the example of the Judaizers to teach all of us a deeper truth about the nature of justification and works. The works that justify us (as we saw in Romans 2:6–11) are works done *in Christ*. When the Judaizers were saying we had to go back to the Old Covenant in order to be saved, they were, in essence, saying Christ and the New Covenant weren't enough. In so doing, they rejected Jesus Christ and the New Covenant. Jesus said, "I am the way, the truth, and the life; no one comes to the Father, but by me." The Judaizers were attempting to be justified *apart from Christ*. St. Paul's point is that we can only perform salvific acts *in Christ*! If we're not "in Christ," even our outwardly "righteous deeds" will avail us nothing.

Further, notice Romans 2:4: Before St. Paul even talks about the works we must do in order to be saved, he says, "Do you not know that God's kindness is meant to lead you to repentance?" It's only God's kindness that leads us to repentance so that we *can* perform good works. Once we are in Christ, we must perform good works in order to *remain* in Christ. And how do we get in Christ, according to St. Paul? Through baptism:

> Do you not know that all of us who have been baptized into Christ Jesus were baptized into his death? We were buried therefore with him by baptism into death, so that as Christ was raised from the dead by the glory of the Father, we too might *walk in newness of life* [Rom. 6:3–4].

You emphasize to Martin the fact that the Scriptures and the Catholic Church teach that it's only works done in Christ after baptism that justify the believer. And they must be done in cooperation with God's grace and not by one's own power as the Judaizers were performing them. This is precisely what St. Paul teaches in Galatians 3:2–3, 5:2–6. He writes concerning these same "Judaizers:"

> Let me ask you only this: Did you receive the Spirit by *works of the law*, or by hearing with faith? Are you so foolish? Having begun with the Spirit, are you now ending with the flesh? . . . Now I, Paul, say to you that if you receive circumcision, Christ will be of no advantage to you. I testify again to every man who receives circumcision that he is bound to keep the whole law. You are severed from Christ, you who would be justified by the law; *you have fallen away from grace.* For through the Spirit, by faith, we wait for the hope of righteousness [Greek: *dikaiosoune* — justification]. For *in Christ Jesus* neither circumcision nor uncircumcision is of any avail, *but faith working through love.*

Notice St. Paul's emphasis on our being in grace and our working through the Spirit and in Christ. Back in Romans, St. Paul says similarly that once we're in Christ, we must choose to remain in him:

"Therefore, since we are justified by faith, we have peace with God through our Lord Jesus Christ. Through him we have obtained access to this *grace in which we stand* and we rejoice in our hope of sharing the glory of God" (Rom. 5:1–2).

There is no such notion as "justification by faith alone" with St. Paul. In Romans 6:16, St. Paul tells us that after baptism (remember Romans 6:3–4?), *obedience to Christ* (that means good works!) leads us to justification, while sin (that means bad works!) will lead us to death:

"Do you not know that if you yield yourselves to any

one as obedient slaves, you are slaves of the one whom you obey, either of sin, which leads to death, or of obedience, which leads to righteousness?" [Greek: *eis dikaiosunen* — unto justification].

Notice that St. Paul makes it very clear. Obedience leads to justification and eternal life while sin leads to eternal death (see also Romans 6:23). But his emphasis isn't just on works, but works done *in and through the power of Christ.* In Romans 8:1–14, St. Paul tells us in no uncertain terms that we must be in Christ in order to do works that please God:

> There is therefore now no condemnation for those who are in Christ Jesus. . . . [W]ho walk not according to the flesh but according to the Spirit. . . . [A]nd those who are in the flesh cannot please God. . . . So, then, brethren, we are debtors, not to the flesh, to live according to the flesh — for if you live according to the flesh you will die, but if by the Spirit you put to death the deeds of the body you will live. For all who are led by the Spirit of God are the sons of God.

The key is to remember St. Paul is emphasizing our continuing in Christ, in His grace or "kindness" as the Apostle says in Romans 11:22:

"Note then the kindness and the severity of God: severity toward those who have fallen, but God's kindness to you, *provided you continue in his kindness*; otherwise you too will be cut off."

Just so no one gets the wrong idea of what St. Paul is saying, he puts it plain and simple in Galatians 5:19–21 and 6:7–8. If we allow ourselves to be dominated by our "flesh," or lower nature, we will not make it to heaven (unless, of course, we confess our sins, turn from them, and seek the forgiveness of God).

Now the works of the flesh are plain: immorality, impurity, licentiousness, idolatry, sorcery, enmity, strife, jealousy, anger, selfishness, dissension, party spirit, envy, drunkenness, carousing and the like. I warn you, as I warned you before, that those who do such things shall not inherit the kingdom of God. . . . Do not be deceived; God is not mocked, for whatever a man sows, that he will also reap. For he who sows to his own flesh will from the flesh reap corruption [eternal death]; but he who sows to the Spirit will from the Spirit reap eternal life.

At this point, Martin responds: "But what about Ephesians 2:8–9 which says 'For by grace you have been saved through faith; and this is not your own doing, it is the gift of God — *not because of works*, lest any man should boast.'"

## Step Three

You respond by showing him the context of Ephesians 2:8–9. In verses 4–6 St. Paul says:

"But God, who is rich in mercy, out of the great love with which he loved us, even when we were dead through our trespasses, made us alive together with Christ . . . and raised us up with him. . . ."

Here, St. Paul is talking about the initial grace of salvation or justification by which we're raised from death unto life. We already said this grace is *entirely* unmerited. My heavens, the Catholic Church baptizes babies! How much more can she do to demonstrate this truth. What kind of works could a newborn baby have done to merit anything? However, once that baby grows up and reaches the age of accountability, he or she must begin to "work out [his or her] own salvation with fear and trembling; for God is at work in [him or her], both to will and to work for his good pleasure" (Phil. 2:12–13). Or, as St. Paul says in Ephesians 2:10, the very next verse after the one Martin quoted, "For we are his workmanship, created in Christ Jesus for good works, which God prepared beforehand, that we should walk in them."

You sum it up: "In the final analysis, I think Father McDuff made a great point when he quoted James 2:24. Are we justified by faith? Certainly! But by faith *alone*? No way! "You see that a man is justified by works and not by faith alone."

Jesus says it similarly. Are we saved by faith in Jesus? Certainly! John 11:25: "I am the resurrection and the life; he who believes in me, though he die, yet shall he live." Are we saved by faith *alone*? No way! In Matthew 19:17–19, Jesus says, "If you would enter life, keep the commandments. . . You shall not kill, You shall not commit adultery, you shall not steal, You shall not bear false witness, Honor your father and mother, and, You shall love your neighbor as yourself."

As you finish quoting these last verses, you're pleasantly surprised to hear Martin say, "You've made some very good points and given me much to think about. Thank you very much." You respond with a handshake and a smile. Turning back to the rest of the gathered group, you declare, "The next round of doughnuts and coffee are on me!"

# 13

# Can an All-Good God Exist?

*Here's what to say when someone calls*
*God "Dr. Evil" (that's right, baby)*

## Scenario

You're finally going for it! After twenty-five years, you're going back to school for that B.A. you've always wanted. The plan is to spend two years at a community college, then transfer to a university.

In your first semester, you take a philosophy course entitled, "A Seminar on the Problem of Good and Evil." Sounds interesting. Maybe the class will give the classic Christian perspective on the topic. It may also provide an opportunity to share the Catholic Faith.

You soon find that the only perspective being explored belongs to Professor Austin Bowers: a 1960s throwback, with bad hair and bad philosophy. Austin — as he insists on being called — not only claims that an all-powerful God does not exist, he claims God *cannot* exist because of the reality of evil in the world.

Austin rephrases the question skeptics have asked for centuries. He puts it this way: "Suppose a baby crawled out into the street, with a speeding car heading toward him. A man standing nearby, close enough to save the baby without any risk to himself, does nothing. He watches the baby die. We would consider such a man scum! Well, if God existed, he would have been in the same position to help billions of people throughout the centuries. Yet, he has done nothing! He is either *unable* to prevent evil — if so he's not all-powerful. Or he is *unwilling* to prevent evil — if so, he's not all-good." Austin then claims that if God were indeed the source of all that exists, He would *have* to be the ultimate source of evil. And if He is the source of evil, He cannot be all-good.

You find it very difficult to get a word in during Austin's lectures. From day to day, he consistently ridicules the Christian God — in particular, he targets the "Catholic notion" of an all-powerful God. He gives overt preference to other religions, such as Buddhism, which doesn't claim to have an answer for the origin of evil at all. Gautama ("the Buddha") taught that "existence is suffering." Evil simply exists. One simply accepts this as fact and doesn't attempt to solve the problem of evil's origin. You notice that Austin likes any philosophy or religion that teaches one *cannot know* ultimate truth. If anyone makes the claim of having the truth, he is no friend of Professor Austin Bowers. "The only thing we can know with certainty is that we cannot know anything with certainty," seems to be Austin's basic but unadmitted philosophy.

As the weeks pass, you notice Austin is having considerable influence on the young college freshmen in your class. Though his arguments are lame, his charismatic personality and command of words are persuasive. The authoritative tone of his British accent seems to be impressing them as well. You say to yourself, "Who in the world is Austin Bowers, that he should be allowed to go on this way unchallenged?" You realize you must speak up and bring some sanity to this discussion. One day, during a lecture on the nature of evil, you raise your hand and Austin gives you time to speak. Nervously, you make the point that he has articulated his and other views on the problem of evil, but hasn't presented an accurate Christian perspective. When he claims he has, you insist he was inaccurate in his presentation. Fearing you'll be cut off at any moment, you launch into a defense of the Catholic position.

## Step One

You explain that Austin's first error is in presenting evil as if it has substance. If it did, then one could say God created it, because God created all substance *ex nihilo* (out of nothing). However, evil does not have substance. It only exists as the *lack of some good*.

Evil — be it physical or moral — exists as *a real privation*. "Privation" is by definition *the lack of something*. For example, blindness is a physical evil. But what is blindness? The *absence of* sight in a body which ought to have it. We use the term *real* in "real privation" because, though evil has no substance of its own, it is still very real. Christian Science, and other cults, erroneously teach that evil is mere illusion. Anyone suffering a serious ailment knows this is not the case.

Moral evil is only found in beings endowed with freedom. It is defined as *the absence of right order* in some performed action which *ought* to have right order. Once again, we see that moral evil — like physical evil — has no substance of its own, but is actually the *lack of something*. It is the lack of some perfection which ought to be present.

For example, the man who commits adultery *fails* to put God, his wife and the marriage covenant before a relationship with another woman. There are many imperfections involved with this action, among them are lust, infidelity, a lack of love for God and a lack of love for spouse. God certainly is not the creator of moral evil, here. He created perfect order in marriage. The adulterer chooses to act out of order.

To understand the nature of evil, we must go back to the beginning. In the Book of Genesis, God created everything good. One particular good He created is called free will. That good became involved with the entrance of evil into the world, not because of anything God did, but because of choices made by free moral agents named Adam and Eve. They chose to abuse the gift God gave them. It is wrong to blame God for the free acts of humans.

Surprised that Austin is giving you so much time, you see an opportunity to share the Faith with the entire class. You make the point that God only permitted that evil at all because, being all-good and all-powerful, He knew that He would cause a greater good to rise out of that evil. You then tell them that God Himself was committed to bringing that greater good about through His own sacrifice on the cross.

Just then, Austin breaks in and claims this to be just another example of Christianity's many contradictions. He says, "You assert God is not the cause of evil in the world, and yet we see example after example in the Bible of God causing all sorts of evils." He mentions the famous ten plagues everyone remembers Charlton Heston calling down upon Yul Brynner in "The Ten Commandments" (Ex. 7:11). He mentions God killing the Egyptians in the Red Sea (Ex. 14:27–28). Same movie! Then, he surprises you by mentioning Ananias and Sapphira in the New Testament (Acts 5:1–10). You didn't think he knew the Bible well enough to bring up that one.

Just when you're ready to respond, the time for the class runs out and you have to leave. You can't wait to come back for the next class.

## Step Two

Two or three minutes into Austin's next lecture, you pick up where you left off. This class is becoming a dialogue between you and Professor Bowers! You explain to Austin and the whole class that when God created the world, He created everything *good*. He was not the cause of evil. In fact, God can never be the cause of *moral* evil. Because He has no imperfection in Him, He could never choose to act immorally. He could have created Adam and Eve as robots, but He chose to give them free will. At this point, you turn to the class and ask them, "How many of you would rather be robots?" As you notice the majority of the students nodding in agreement with you, you continue. "In the last class, Austin gave examples of physical evils caused by God in Scripture. These examples of God inflicting punishment on humanity involve no moral evil at all. These are examples of God's *justice*. Justice is good!"

You explain that, in the beginning, there was no evil or pain at all. It was only after the fall of Adam and Eve, as Scripture says, that sin and death entered the world (Rom. 5:12, 1 Tim. 2:14). Original sin damaged human nature, so that all of Adam and Eve's progeny would be born with a "fallen" nature — essentially good, but tainted by sin — its intellect darkened and its will weakened.

Even creation itself is in a fallen state (Rom. 8:20–23) and awaits the final redemption when all things will be restored, and there will be a "new heaven and a new earth." (Rev. 21:1) Hence, we have earthquakes, floods, etc. We must consider the damage sin caused (and continues to cause) once it entered the picture. And we must consider things like justice, reward and punishment. This is the context in which God causes or permits physical evils in the world. Because of the disorder of sin, punishment and pain happen in the name of justice and in the name of love. We are no longer in the Garden of Eden. In explaining what he called "the problem of pain," C. S. Lewis used the relationship between a father and son to illustrate this point. At times, the father must "spare not the rod" (Prov. 13:24) in raising a son if he truly loves him. It is difficult for a father to cause pain to a son; yet, if he does not discipline the child, he will hurt him far worse in the long run. The child will develop bad habits and character flaws that could lead to his spiritual demise.

God causes or permits physical evils in the world — whether they are caused by the free acts of man's fallen nature or by His direct intervention — only inasmuch as He foresees a greater good coming out of them. As for moral evils — which are caused only by the free acts of rational creatures — God allows them to occur only because He can foresee greater good rising out of them, as well.

Austin responds by saying, "I don't think we can compare a father spanking a child to an earthquake causing the death of thousands of people. *Innocent people* are killed in these disasters. They don't deserve this kind of spanking!"

## Step Three

You hear a chuckle from the class as you respond. "There are two reasons we inflict punishment upon people in this world. First, to punish for wrongdoing. Second, in order to rehabilitate the offender." You go on to explain that the severity of punishment is determined by the seriousness of the offense or offenses. We determine the degree of seriousness by examining the nature of the offense and the identity of its victim. For example, the punishment for stealing a cookie from a cookie jar is different than the punishment for robbing a bank. Killing a dog results in a different punishment than killing a human being does. A human being has immeasurably more dignity than a dog; therefore, a crime against a man deserves much more serious punishment.

God is *infinite* in dignity; therefore, an offense against Him requires infinite punishment or infinite atonement. Anything we experience by way of pain in this life is a mercy, compared to what we truly deserve for just one offense against an infinitely holy God! When we see how serious our offenses against an infinitely holy God are, we will no longer have a problem with our own suffering. We deserve worse than what we experience no matter how difficult our situation may be.

Responding to the problem of the suffering of the innocent, you note that we are a human family. And as a family we affect one another. We see this vividly in the news, when we hear of "crack babies" being born drug-addicted because of the sins of their mothers. We also see how the sins of our culture affect an entire generation. The loss of any sense of morality in education, government and the media has led to a generation that has lost its way, that has taken to manifesting its lack of direction in increasing promiscuity, crime and violence. On a spiritual level, our sins have an even more profound effect. Our sins not only affect us, but all of humanity.

Our sufferings, whether brought on by ourselves or by some other member of the human family, are not without purpose. They are opportunities for conversion, healing and atonement that can only come through suffering (See 2 Cor. 1:5–7, 2 Cor. 12:8–10, Rom. 8:17).

Seeing that the clock on the wall is ticking down the last few minutes of class, you urge your classmates to consider the nature of our sins. They are committed against an infinite God and, therefore, require infinite reparation. Only God has the power to supply that kind of atonement. No matter how much we were to suffer, we could never atone for an infinite offense because we do not have an infinite nature. However, when we see that God Himself has become one of us in Jesus Christ and *innocently* suffered for the entire human family, we finally have the answer for the problem of evil and human suffering. There is purpose in suffering, and that purpose is to achieve salvation. Jesus was the only one able to *infinitely* atone for our *infinite* transgressions against an *infinitely* holy God (2 Cor. 5:21). Now, he calls us, *in Him*, to join our sufferings with His and help heal the world (Luke 9:23, Col. 1:24, 1 Peter 2:21–24).

We cannot do that on our own. But through baptism we are incorporated into the Body of Christ (Rom. 6:3–4, 1 Cor. 12:12–27), thus our sufferings become salvific because they are joined with His. Turning to the class, you make this final comment: "The cross of Jesus Christ is the only thing that makes sense of the problem of evil. And it is the only thing that can give lasting peace and hope in the midst of the reality of the pain we know and experience in the world."

## Step Four

From that day on, you continue to defend the Catholic position on the nature of good and evil, the existence of God and other points that arise. Austin picks on the Catholic Faith again and again in his lectures. It's obvious to everyone that his attacks are aimed at you. One day, you discover the reason why. You sit down with Austin in the cafeteria and begin to make small talk. Sure enough, a discussion of the Catholic Faith ensues. Right in the middle of your response to one of his diatribes against the Church, he interjects, "Well, I guess I'm going to hell, then. I was married in the Church, got divorced and remarried outside of the Church."

Beneath the cloak of intellectual reasoning against the existence of God, you often discover a moral dilemma. There is frequently much pain and anger clouding the reason of the skeptic. However, in order to get to the real source of the problem, one must first penetrate the intellectual facade.

You try to help Austin, perhaps recommending a good priest for him to see, but he doesn't want to talk any more. You have to leave him in the hands of our Lord and our Lady. But what a lesson in the importance of sharing the Faith even with those who seem to be the most antagonistic.

# 14

# Chicken Soup for the Evangelical Soul

*A Jewish mother knows just what*
*this Bible-believing pastor needs*

## Scenario

Mike, an Evangelical Protestant pastor, heads into a Catholic bookstore one afternoon, curious to discover what Catholics could possibly say to defend their religion. As he flips through a Catholic liturgical calendar, he notices that the feast day of the "Solemnity of Mary" is celebrated on January 1. Not being familiar with "feast days," and knowing even less about what Catholics believe about Mary, he asks the young woman at the counter what the title "Solemnity of Mary" refers to. She explains that it is the day on which the Church celebrates the fact that Mary is the "Mother of God."

Frowning, he asks the woman to show him any books that could explain and defend that notion in detail. She takes him to a large section of apologetics books and tapes, and after browsing for half an hour, he leaves the store with an armload of books and tape sets.

Two weeks later, Pastor Mike calls Gary, a friend of his

who is the pastor of another large Evangelical church in town. He asks if he'd like to get together and help him research some questions he has about the Catholic Church.

"Sure, Mike," Gary says over the phone. "I'd be happy to help out. As it happens, I am preparing a series of teachings on Roman Catholicism for our Sunday service. We need to help our people see the errors of Roman Catholicism, not just to keep them from that heresy, but to equip them to minister to their Catholic friends and family members." The two ministers set a date and time for their meeting.

## The Plan

When they meet over coffee, Pastor Mike explains he's been studying the Catholic teaching on Mary as the Mother of God. "This is starting to make sense to me," he adds hesitantly. "I'd like to know what you think about the Catholic case, Gary."

"Sure, but before we get into that," Gary says earnestly, "Let's keep in mind three basic points. First, the obvious. Nowhere in Scripture do we find the words 'Mother of God' used to describe Mary. If this doctrine were as important as Roman Catholics claim, wouldn't at least one of the biblical writers have used it?

"Two, Luke 1:43 seems to be the only verse of Scripture that Catholics use to support their claim. This is the account of the visitation of Mary to her much older cousin Elizabeth. When Mary enters into her cousin's home, Elizabeth exclaims with a loud cry, 'Blessed are you among women, and blessed is the fruit of your womb! And why is this granted me, that the mother of my Lord should come to me?'"

Gary continues. "Notice, the text does not call Mary

'Mother of God,' it calls her 'mother of my *Lord.*' As we both know, Mike, the New Testament uses the term 'lord' in the context of divinity at times, but it also uses the term in the context of other authority. For example, in 1 Corinthians 8:5, St. Paul writes: 'indeed there are many "gods" and many "lords."' This is an obvious instance of 'lord' not being used as referring to divinity.

"And the third point to remember," Gary adds, "is that it would be impossible for God to have a Mother! The fact that Catholics claim Mary to be the Mother of God is complete blasphemy! God is Trinity. If Mary is the Mother of God, she is the mother of the Trinity. Therefore, the Trinity is no longer a Trinity, it is a 'quadrinity!' Mary would have to be God herself if she is the source of the life of the Godhead." Gary smiles and sits back confidently.

## The Response

Pastor Mike begins nervously. "Gary, I think we should think about a few things before we proceed."

"Okay, Mike. Like what?"

At this point, Pastor Mike begins to share some interesting material he has discovered in his research. First, he urges Pastor Gary to reconsider his first point. "To say Mary cannot be the Mother of God because sacred Scripture does not use those explicit words is not the way we want to go. We would then have to conclude the Trinity to be false, because that word is not found in Holy Writ either. The question we need to ask is: Is the *concept* of Mary, Mother of God, taught in Sacred Scripture?"

"As far as your second point is concerned, I think we might want to consider a few things in regard to that, too.

The title 'Lord,' is a title of divinity for Jesus in the New Testament. In 1 Corinthians 8:5, you were correct in pointing out the fact that the term 'Lord' (Greek: *kurios*) was not used to refer to divinity. However, the very next verse says: 'Yet to us there is one God, the Father, from whom are all things, and for whom we exist, and one *Lord*, Jesus Christ, through whom are all things and through whom we exist.' Notice the connection between Jesus being 'Lord' and His being creator of all things. This unequivocally identifies 'Lord' as referring to Christ's divinity, just as John 1:1–3 connects Jesus as 'God' (Greek: *theos*) to His being the Creator of all things: 'In the beginning was the Word, and the Word was with God, and the Word was God. He was in the beginning with God; all things were made through him, and without him was not anything made that was made.'

"Genesis 1:1 cannot make it any more clear that it is almighty God who is the creator of all things. The title *kurios*, applied to Christ as Creator of all things in 1 Corinthians 8:6, is clearly a title of divinity for Christ.

"Another of the many examples the Catholics could cite is Mark 2:28: 'So the Son of man is lord even of the sabbath.' These words were packed for our Lord's first-century Jewish audience. Jesus called Himself the Lord of the Sabbath. In the Old Testament, it is Yahweh alone who is Lord of the Sabbath" (cf. Exodus 16:23, 16:25, 20:10, Deut. 5:14).

Pastor Gary, a little wary now, asks, "What are you saying to me, Mike? Do you believe Mary is the Mother of God?"

Avoiding a direct answer, Pastor Mike continues, "Listen to what the *Catechism of the Catholic Church* says in paragraph 495:

Called in the Gospels "the mother of Jesus," Mary is ac-
claimed by Elizabeth, at the prompting of the Spirit and
even before the birth of her son, as "the mother of my
Lord." In fact, the One Whom she conceived as man by
the Holy Spirit, Who truly became her Son according to
the flesh, was none other than the Father's eternal Son,
the second person of the Holy Trinity. Hence the Church
confesses that Mary is truly "Mother of God" (*Theotokos*).

"Here the Catholic Church is saying Mary is the Mother
of God precisely because Jesus Christ, her Son, is Himself God. I have to admit, Gary, I'm having a hard time
disagreeing with that. The *Catechism* here references the
Council of Ephesus (A.D. 431). When I researched the
Council of Ephesus, I found a number of very important
things. In the first of the many anathemas of St. Cyril,
bishop of Alexandria, accepted by the Council, we find:

> If anyone does not confess that God is truly Emmanuel,
> and that on this account the Holy Virgin is the Mother of
> God (for according to the flesh she gave birth to the Word
> of God become flesh by birth), let him be anathema.

"Far from just referencing one verse, as you mentioned at
the beginning of our conversation, the Council here refers
to the prophecy of Isaiah 7:14. The Messiah was to be born
of a woman, and yet would be 'God with us.' And it doesn't
stop there. St. Cyril and the fathers of this Council referred
to a host of Scriptures. On page 25 of the book *The Mother
of God*, Valentine Long, O.F.M. writes:

> St. Cyril had a wide choice of utterances from our blessed
> Lord to rely upon. Never once in the Gospels did Christ,
> who in word and deed revealed his two natures, speak as
> two persons. It was "Young man, I say to you, arise," and
> not "the God in me" says so. He did not ask the blind
> men before their instantaneous cure, "Do you believe my

divine omnipotence can do this?" No, it was simply; "Do you believe that I am able to do this?" Dying on the Cross, the Savior did not cry out that his human nature thirsted. His words were, "I thirst." His divinity worked miracles; his humanity needed to eat and drink and sleep, but the "I" of his assertions, which admitted both natures, allowed no duality of person. "The Father and I are one" and "The Father is greater than I" are expressions of the same undivided person.

"The bottom line is, Gary, we create two persons when we say Mary is the mother of the *man* Jesus, but not the *divine* Jesus. Colossians 2:9 says 'in him the whole fullness of deity dwells bodily.' And Colossians 1:16 says 'in him all things were created, in heaven and on earth, visible and invisible.' These texts do not say 'in *Them*,' they say 'in *Him*.' As I'm starting to realize, this is serious business, because we are talking about different Christs. He is either one Person or two."

Pastor Gary is a bit shell-shocked. "But Mike, if the Catholic Church claims Mary is the Mother of God, wouldn't that make her divine? God is Father, Son and Holy Spirit. If Mary were the Mother of God, she would have to be the mother of the Father, the Son and the Holy Spirit, right?"

"Actually, Gary, remember what the *Catechism* said in paragraph 495. It said that Mary is only the Mother of the second Person of the Trinity, by virtue of the Incarnation. The Father and the Holy Spirit were not incarnated."

"Okay, I can see your point," Gary admits reluctantly, "but even if she is only the mother of the second Person, He is just as eternal as the other two divine Persons in the Trinity. So Mary would still have to be eternal in order to be Christ's mother."

"As I understand it, Gary, the Catholic Church isn't

saying that Mary is the source of the *divine* nature of the second Person of the Trinity. I listened to some Catholic apologetics tapes by a former Protestant who used the example of a family to show how Mary can be the Mother of God. He explained that when a man and a woman have a child, their child has a body and a soul. They are not the *source* of its soul — God is, because He directly creates the baby's soul and infuses it into the body at the moment of conception. But even though God is the source of the child's immortal soul, nobody would conclude that the child's mother is merely the mother of his body. She is his mother *completely*, because mothers don't give birth to bodies, they give birth to *persons*.

"In the same way, while Mary wasn't the *source* of Christ's divine nature or His human soul, she was still His mother in the fullest sense. Christ's divine nature didn't change at the Incarnation. The divine nature can't change, as the Bible says it can't in Malachi 3:6, Numbers 23:19 and James 1:17. Christ's human and divine natures were completely united in the Incarnation, and Mary gave birth to this divine Person. Anyway, that's the Catholic position in a nutshell, and as you can tell, I've become rather sympathetic to it."

Pastor Gary struggles for words. "Well, I'm not ready to say that Mary is the Mother of God, but maybe we can move on to another issue. If Mary is indeed the Mother of God, we still have the problem of Catholic excess. They go from calling Mary the Mother of God to calling her *their* mother, and they tend to worship her as if she were herself divine. That's a problem."

"Let me show you a few things I've discovered in my reading of Catholic books," Mike says. He's more and more comfortable with explaining this Catholic teaching, and he can see that the more he explains it, the more clearly Gary sees it, too. This is obviously making his friend uncomfortable, as his anti-Catholic presuppositions are being shaken, but he feels compelled to press on. "First, the Catholic Church doesn't teach or condone the worship of Mary. Rather, it teaches that she should be *honored*, in keeping with the commandment, 'Honor your father and mother.' If Mary is the Mother of Jesus, and we are His adopted brothers and sisters, as it says in Romans 8:14–17 and Galatians 4:4–6, wouldn't that naturally imply that she is our mother, too? And if so, shouldn't we all obey Scripture's command to honor her?"

"But Mike!" Gary exclaims. "She's *dead*! And you know as well as I do that Deuteronomy 18:10–11 condemns necromancy and contact with the dead. And that's exactly what Catholics do when they pray to Mary!"

"That's what I always thought, too. But look at the context of Deuteronomy 18. It's a condemnation of the use of mediums, wizards and witches. In other words, it forbids communication with the *spiritually* dead. Luke 20:38 says that those who die in Christ are alive in the spirit in Him. There are plenty of biblical examples of living Christians having contact with the saints in heaven. Take a look at Matthew 17:1–3, where Peter, James and John are brought into contact *by Christ* with Moses and Elijah on the Mount of Transfiguration."

"Hold on," Gary says. "Let's slow down. I need time to think about all this. Why don't we switch to another topic for now? We can talk about this 'Mother of God' issue more some other time." A wide smile comes over his face. "Say! Why don't we discuss the errors of the Catholic Church on salvation, their 'works righteousness' system of justification, how they don't have an absolute assurance of salvation the way Christians do, and their mistake in teaching that . . ."

Pastor Mike interrupts with his own smile. "Funny you should mention that. It just so happens I've been studying some Catholic books and tapes on that very subject." Mike opens his well-worn Bible to the book of Ephesians. "Here, let me show you what Catholics believe about salvation."

Pastor Gary looks nervously at his watch, and begins to wiggle like the worms in the can he just opened.

# About the Author

Tim Staples is a convert to the Catholic Church from Protestantism. Schooled in the Assemblies of God denomination, he once had studied to become a minister and took courses at the Jimmy Swaggart College, where he came into contact with just about every anti-Catholic argument imaginable. After converting to the Catholic Church, he became active as a full-time apologist, giving seminars, engaging in public debates with Protestant ministers, hosting a popular call-in apologetics radio program, and producing many study tapes on apologetics. He is currently the director of evangelization for the Catholic Resource Center, and he writes the popular "Nuts & Bolts" column in *Envoy* magazine. A catalog of Tim's tapes are available by calling 626-331-3549.

# Recommended Reading

*A Father Who Keeps His Promises*, Scott Hahn (Servant).

*Surprised by Truth: 11 Converts Give the Biblical and Historical Reasons for Becoming Catholic*, Patrick Madrid (Basilica Press).

*Rome Sweet Home*, Scott & Kimberly Hahn (Ignatius Press).

*Pope Fiction: Answers to 30 Myths and Misconceptions About the Papacy*, Patrick Madrid (Basilica Press).

*Making Senses Out of Scripture*, Mark Shea (Basilica Press).

*Springtime of Evangelization*, Pope John Paul II, introduced by Thomas Williams, L.C. (Basilica Press).

*Theology and Sanity*, Frank Sheed (Ignatius Press).

*Theology for Beginners*, Frank Sheed (Servant Press).

*By What Authority? An Evangelical Discovers Tradition*, Mark Shea (Our Sunday Visitor).

*Upon This Rock*, Stephen K. Ray (Ignatius Press).

*Any Friend of God's Is a Friend of Mine*, Patrick Madrid (Basilica Press).

*Not by Scripture Alone*, Robert Sungenis, Patrick Madrid, et al. (Queenship).

*Tradition & Traditions*, Yves M. J. Congar (Basilica Press).

*Mary and the Fathers of the Church*, Luigi Gambero (Ignatius Press).

*Catholic for a Reason*, Leon Suprenant, Scott Hahn, et al. (Emmaus Road).

*The Fathers of the Church*, Mike Aquilina (Our Sunday Visitor).

*Jesus, Peter & the Keys*, David Hess, et al., (Queenship).

# If you want to be filled by the Holy Spirit, He needs an opening.

# Being in the audio tape business, that opening seems obvious.

O kay, so we can't guarantee that if you listen to our ten exciting new tape sets you'll be filled with the Holy Spirit, but we can guarantee that when you listen you *will* be able to hear every word. Because at Basilica Press we think the fantastic quality of our content deserves quality reproduction using top quality tapes.

Our tape sets include lively new Catholic/Protestant debates, seminars and conferences featuring popular speakers and veteran apologists Curtis Martin, Jeff Cavins, Dr. Scott Hahn and Patrick Madrid. Learn apologetics do's and don'ts, how to handle difficult questions, how to love others the way God loves you, and much more. And if you're *not* filled with the Holy Spirit when you're through, well, you'll at least be closer to Christ and a *lot* more knowledgeable about your Catholic Faith. (Such a deal!)

BASILICA ™

P R E S S

*Bringing Christ to the World*

**Faith, Hope & Charity**
*Jeff Cavins*
Three inspiring and
exciting talks on the
importance of the
virtues of faith, hope
and charity, and how to
live them more deeply
in your daily life.
**$19.99**

**Speak the Truth in Love**
*Patrick Madrid*
A fast-paced intro-
duction to the do's
and don'ts of
Catholic apologetics
and evangelization.
Learn to explain,
defend and share
your Catholic Faith.
**$34.99**

**Winning Souls — Not Just Arguments**
*Curtis Martin &
Patrick Madrid*
An exciting apologet-
ics and evangelization
seminar. Topics
include Mary, the role
of Scripture in the
Church, justification
and the Eucharist.
**$24.99**

**Search the Scriptures**
*Patrick Madrid vs.
Dr. Rowland Ward*
A new
Catholic/Protestant
debate.
Topic one: Is the
Bible the only infalli-
ble rule of faith?
Topic two: What must
we do to be saved?
**$24.99**

**Hold Fast to the Traditions You Were Taught**
*Patrick Madrid vs.
Rev. Fred Needham*
• Is there evidence for
Catholic teachings on
Tradition and the
Magisterium? • Is the
Doctrine of the Holy
Eucharist what Christ
taught? • Q & A session
with the audience
**$19.99**

**Defending the Faith**
*Patrick Madrid*
Tape 1: Common
mistakes Catholics
make when
sharing the Faith.
Tape 2: Apologetics
workshop on
explaining the com-
munion of saints.
**$11.99**

**What Still Divides Us?**
*Patrick Madrid, et. al.*
A dramatic, eye-open-
ing Catholic/Protestant
debate on the two
central slogans of the
Protestant
Reformation: *Sola
Scriptura* and *Sola
Fide.*
**$49.99**

**Handling Difficult Questions**
*Patrick Madrid*
Practical informa-
tion from
a veteran Catholic
apologist on how to
deal effectively and
charitibly with
difficult questions
about the
Catholic Faith.
**$24.99**

**Surprised by Truth**
*Patrick Madrid*
Why are so many
Protest-ants becom-
ing Catholic? An
insightful, humor-
ous and challenging
look at why many
people are convert-
ing to the Catholic
Church.
**$5.99**

**Like Father, Like Son**
*Scott Hahn, Ph.D.*
Brand new! One of
the most exciting
talks of his career.
A rousing and
deeply personal
teaching on the
nature and meaning
of fatherhood
**$11.99**

**"I'm Not Being Fed!"**
*Jeff Cavins*
In Tape 1, Jeff
answers the often
heard expression
"I left the Catholic
Church because I
wasn't being fed."
In Tape 2, he
chronicles his
moving journey
back to the
Catholic Church.
**2 Cassettes
$11.99**

**The Hour of Christ**
*Dr. Scott Hahn*
NEW! A moving
and inspiring talk
on the sacrifice
Jesus Christ made
to free us from
the chains of
sin and death.
**2 Cassettes
$11.99**

**What is Purgatory?**
*Patrick Madrid*
This step-by-step
explanation leads
you through the
basic elements of
the doctrine of pur-
gatory: what it is,
what it's not, and
where it's found in
Scripture
**1 Cassette
$5.99**

**Keeping Your Kids Catholic**
*Marcus Grodi*
Marcus Grodi, a
well-known
Catholic leader,
delivers a rich and
insightful array of
practical advice,
pastoral insights
and solid Catholic
principles.
**2 Cassettes
$11.99**

# "Man Shall not Live by Bread Alone..."

## Dr. Scott Hahn and Jeff Cavins

@*Home with the Word*

*J*esus spent forty days fasting in the desert, with the Devil tempting Him to turn stones into loaves of bread. Jesus responded, "Man shall not live by bread alone, but by every word that proceeds from the mouth of God" (Matthew 4:4).

Earthly food keeps our bodies running but, like our bodies, it's perishable. Our souls, however, are immortal. They need immortal sustenance: the life-giving Word of God.

The Missionaries of Faith Foundation is excited to bring you the Word of God in a new, powerful weekly Internet Bible study conducted by Dr. Scott Hahn and Jeff Cavins. It's called @*Home with the Word*.

@*Home with the Word* is ideal for both group and individual study. Each week Scott Hahn and Jeff Cavins present a passage from the Bible, along with its historical background. They provide tips for understanding the meaning of the passage and make important connections to the Catechism of the Catholic Church, papal writings, the Church Fathers, and the Saints. The program also provides discussion questions, which you can explore on your own or as part of a group.

### @*Home with the Word* also provides:

**Family Night:** This user-friendly weekly program helps families come together to study the Word of God, and discuss important issues facing today's Catholic family. Family activity suggestions also help to bring God's Word home to you and your children.

**Parish Partnership:** Everyone in your parish can benefit from this program. It features free homily help for priests, a listing of Bible studies in your area, and a question & answer forum called **Truth Tracts**. Your questions about the Bible and the Church are answered by Dr. Hahn, Jeff Cavins, Mark Shea, Patrick Madrid, Matthew Pinto, and other Missionaries of Faith Foundation staff members.

The monthly cost for @*Home with the Word* is just $7.

**For more information, call the Missionaries of Faith Foundation at (888) 41-FAITH (888-413-2494) or subscribe at www.moff.org.**

**Missionaries** of **Faith**
FOUNDATION